hope you [will] miss you

[enjoy] you read about

my journey !

Teresa Prins Hood

Saint Somebody

TERESA PRINS-WOOD

WestBow
PRESS
A DIVISION OF THOMAS NELSON
& ZONDERVAN

WestBow Press books may be ordered through booksellers or by contacting:

WestBow Press
A Division of Thomas Nelson & Zondervan
1663 Liberty Drive
Bloomington, IN 47403
www.westbowpress.com
1 (866) 928-1240

ISBN: 978-1-4908-8211-6 (sc)

Library of Congress Control Number: 2015908627

Print information available on the last page.

WestBow Press rev. date: 06/02/2015

CONTENTS

🕊 🕊 🕊

INTRODUCTION

When you look at a statue that is carved out of wood, a statue that you have looked at every Sunday for more than one hundred Sundays, and if the eyes of the statue suddenly begin to move – I'd call that a miracle, wouldn't you? It makes no difference whether you are young or old. A miracle is a miracle.

It's as simple as this: When I was a few months away from turning eight years old, I learned that to become a saint you need to experience three miracles. Yep, just three miracles and the Church would let the whole world know that you are a saint. Your picture would be in books, there would be beautiful statues of you in churches, and you would have your own permanent halo that no one could ever take away.

The starting point of my pursuit for sainthood was in 1961 and it continued into 1969. How is it that I remember the details of a life lived so many decades ago? The answer is how could I possibly forget? Whenever our family made the summertime trek from California to Missouri, for example, I had hour upon hour to think and rethink about my beliefs and my hopes for the future. The eight of us would pile into one of those station wagons where the third seat faces out the back window. As I watched the miles go by, I'd replay the details of my life thus far and make plans for my someday.

By the time I was approaching the fourth grade of elementary school, I already had two miracles under my belt and was waiting for my third. Whenever I was in the presence of a nun or a priest, I would set aside my bashful disposition and in my most confident tone of voice I'd ask if the 'three miracle rule' was true. It may have been my youthful naïveté that caused each and every one of them, without exception, to either nod in the affirmative or to actually put voice to a "yes" that would eventually settle the question in my mind. I had no reason to wonder whether or not they understood my inquiry. I put my faith in their years of devotion to the church and their direct line to God.

And so I waited for miracle number three…

🕊 🕊 🕊

Chapter 1

I KNOW A MIRACLE
WHEN I SEE ONE

I was clueless. There was no advance warning. The sun didn't shine any differently and the sky was as blue and cloudless as the days before. Nothing prepared me for the most spectacular event in my entire eight years on this earth.

The details are as fresh in my mind as if the whole thing happened just last week: Every Sunday morning I walked to church with my two brothers, two sisters, plus Freddy and Trisha from next door. My youngest brother Robby was still too young to walk the six blocks. Lloyd, Lindy, Trisha, and I were getting close to the age when we would be allowed to 'take communion'. The nuns in our catechism classes had instructed us to sit close to the front of the church so that we could watch as communion was served. From our front row pew we could hear as each person receiving weekly communion would say "Lord, I am not worthy that You should come under my roof. Speak but the word and my soul shall be healed". The repetition of those words sounded to me like a song and I could hardly wait for the day to come when I'd be allowed to say them every Sunday morning for the rest of my life.

Children were expected to experience the sacraments of Confession and First Holy Communion prior to entering the fourth grade. Saturday morning catechism classes prepared us for this solemn and festive rite of passage. We'd already learned the critical, unwritten codes of communion conduct:

~ Do not say "hi" to the Altar Boys, even if you know them.
~ Do not open your mouth until the priest gets right up in front of you.
~ Do not stick your tongue out too far or make weird faces.
~ Do not shut your mouth until after the priest has removed his fingers.
~ Do not chomp down on the communion wafer. Doing so is an insult to our Savior.

We'd been told, "Let it melt in your mouth or you might choke on it". We knew that even if we did choke we were not allowed to remove the communion wafer from our mouth. We never dared to ask the consequences of messing up. We may have been young, but we were wise enough to assume the worst.

On the day that the miracle took place, the seven of us sat crowded along the wooden pew that was directly in front of the big statue of Saint Joseph. Joseph held some carpentry tools in one hand and balanced the Baby Jesus on the other arm. Most of the statues in the church were painted in beautiful pastels of pink, peach, pale yellow, blues, and light green with flecks of metallic gold. This particular statue, however, looked as if it had been carved out of wood. It was reddish brown with dark brown streaks. The size of an adult man, Saint Joseph stood in an arched alcove and there was a little spotlight at his feet that shone upward onto his face. Except for looking like it was made of wood, this Joseph was very lifelike.

I liked to imagine how wonderful it would be to be a statue in the front of a church, just standing there looking out at the people. I would not want to appear shy or keep my eyes lowered as most of the statues did. I would want the statue of Saint Me to be looking right out there and I'd have a friendly expression on my face as if I was saying, "Oh, look! You're back again today! I'm so glad you came!" I would want to be wearing a long white gown with a robin-egg blue shawl exactly like the one that The Virgin Mary wore in all her pictures and statues. My arms would be extended as if I was saying, "Come here, come unto me and let me give you a hug."

Mass had just begun. It was Freddy who elbowed my brother Richard and started whispering about something important enough that Richard then passed the word along to the eldest of the group, my sister Sharron. The three of them were sort of bobbing their heads as if some secret music was playing for their ears alone. I noticed that they were looking upward at the Saint Joseph statue.

~~ AND THEN IT HAPPENED ~~

I saw it as well. I saw without having to be told that Saint Joseph's eyes were moving! The four of us were stunned. We sat quietly and swayed our heads from side to side, seeing that as we did, Saint Joseph followed our movements with his gaze. We didn't dare to take our eyes off of him to look at each other or to speak a word. We knew that something incredible was taking place. I knew that this was right up there with multiplying the loaves and fishes, with walking on water, maybe even with raising the dead! This was God showing Himself to us, just to us, through Saint Joseph.

Sharron was in the sixth grade, Richard and Freddy in fourth, and I was eight years old, a third grader. I guess Lindy, Lloyd, and Trisha were one year too young to notice what was going on. I'm sure that God knew they weren't ready for something like this; it might have scared them.

As it turned out, Sharron and I were the brave ones while Richard and Freddy got kind of creeped-out by the whole thing. When mass was over the two boys walked to the front of the church and asked the priest, Father Garon, if they could talk to him. When the magnitude of the experience overwhelmed their ability to speak, Sharron spoke up and informed the priest that either Jesus or Saint Joseph was inside of the statue and that He had been watching us during mass.

Father Garon offered such a kind smile that I wondered if this was not the first time Joseph had behaved in this manner. He told us that the statue had been carved in such a way that wherever you sat or stood, it would appear that

Saint Joseph is following you with his eyes. Apparently, this explanation was sufficient for the rest of the group, but I knew better. I knew that I had never observed this before and that if it had ever happened in the past, I would have noticed.

I thoroughly loved being in the church, looking at the lifelike images; at the little cherubs peering out of the clouds that were painted onto the blue sky ceiling above the gold and white altar area. I had no doubt that this is what Heaven must look like. I knew every inch of the church from the fourteen stained glass Stations of the Cross to the giant Crucifix, to each one of the several statues. I had no doubt that Saint Joseph's eyes had never wandered about as they did on that particular Sunday morning.

When I reported the incident to my mother, she said, "That sounds like a miracle". Those words were all the affirmation my young spirit required. Later that same day I told my best friend Julie about my miracle and she agreed that something very important had happened. Also a third grader, Julie was a purebred Catholic who went to Catholic school. She and her family attended St. James Catholic Church (probably because she was not 'mixed' like those of us who went to public school, Saturday Catechism classes, and attended Mary Star of the Sea Catholic Church). Julie and I became best friends because we were neighbors. We were too young to recognize our differences and she was convinced that I was on my way to sainty greatness.

🕊 🕊 🕊

Chapter 2

A FAITHFUL MIX

Before the miracles ever took place, before I even knew for certain that God wanted me for one of His saints, I knew some things that they didn't know that I knew.

The nuns, the Sisters who taught me Catechism week after week, year after year filled my head with laws and lessons and ideas that formed my character. They instilled into my innocence the beliefs that set me on a path that leads God-ward. At the same time, their wonderful knowledge was sometimes interspersed with notions that I imagined were acceptable to other kids but that just did not fly with me.

For one so quiet and shy who never dared to raise her hand to request permission to ask a question and who only answered aloud when required to do so, I had an unusual confidence about my spiritual future. I had a very personal and unspoken conviction about what was wrong and what was right pertaining to the lessons taught by those who were Holy Ordered to make a Good Catholic out of me. There was no need to debate, I just knew. Well, I suppose there were moments of doubt but God had also blessed me with the creativity to chase those doubts away.

I was the third of six children born to Norma Mary (a purebred Catholic) and Robert E. (not a Catholic) Prins. Because mother had received all of her education in private/parochial schools, it went without saying that her children would be raised Catholic regardless of the fact that it was necessary for us to attend public schools. Throughout our elementary and junior high school years, in order to insure that we received a proper religious upbringing, we were required to spend each Saturday morning at the church along with a large group of other public school children receiving two hours of instruction call Catechism.

We learned some history and rules of the church. We studied the lives of saints and the gory but heroic deaths of the martyrs. We memorized dozens of prayers. We learned about the Holy Days of Obligation when you'd better make it to church or else. We memorized the names of the sacraments in the order in which a person became qualified to receive them.

For youngsters there was infant Baptism, elementary school Confession and First Holy Communion, and then as you prepared for junior high school: Confirmation. The remaining sacraments (Marriage, and Holy Orders) had to wait until you were an adult and, in the case of Xtree Munkshun (the sacrament of Last Rights), until you were on your deathbed. As a little girl, I felt certain that I'd not be receiving the sacrament of Xtree Munkshun until I'd enjoyed many good years of sainthood while living here on earth. (I was fourteen years old before I realized that it is actually called Extreme Unction.)

The one sacrament that held the most prominent place in my young mind was Holy Orders. I liked the sound of it. Holy and Orders. Throughout my years of catechism classes the instructors would address the subject by telling us "you probably won't receive this one-- it is when you become a member of the clergy." They would end this very short portion of lecture by saying "Holy Orders is the sacrament of becoming a nun or a priest." End of lesson. At age seven my best girlfriend told me about the solemn and mysteriously beautiful ritual, equal in importance to an actual wedding ceremony, when a person becomes the Bride of Christ, marrying themselves into the church as a nun or a priest. She never actually attended the ceremony but her aunt had become a nun and Julie thrilled to tell me about the sacrament of Holy Orders.

It looked to me as if parents chose public school for their children if the children were the offspring of a mixed marriage. That's where one parent was Catholic and the other was something else--something that doomed their soul to purgatory at best but most likely to the flames of hell unless they committed themselves to Saturday morning Catechism classes for many, many years. I figured that it was the purebred Catholic child who might someday be invited into the priesthood or the convent. I wondered what my instructors would have thought had I the nerve to stand up and tell them that I had serious intentions of becoming Saint Teresa and, not only that, I also had plans to someday wear the long black habit/gown and cool looking black veil headdress of a nun!

🕊 🕊 🕊

Chapter 3

ANGELS & DEMONS

Catching a glimpse of my reflection in a car window, I wanted to look more angelic than bride dollish. The other girls looked like beautiful, brand new bride dolls. I wanted to look like that Guardian Angel in the picture of the little boy and girl crossing the bridge before a storm.

Decked out in white lace from head to foot, even the lace around my anklet socks made me feel divine. Candles glowed and organ music played as parents, siblings, extended family, neighbors, and friends filled the church on the day that our Catechism class participated in the sacrament of First Holy Communion. Each little girl wore a white dress and a short veil or a mantilla (a round piece of lace that looks like the doily under a table lamp). The boys wore a black suit and most of them wore a bow tie. Our grand entrance into the church was led by the priest, followed by the altar boys, the nuns, and then the children.

Some of the dresses were off-white and some of the veils showed signs of having been mended because it was common practice for every girl in a family to wear the same outfit as a matter of tradition. I was wearing the knee length satin-with-lace-overlay dress and shoulder length veil that my sister Sharron had worn three years earlier. Lindy would wear the outfit next spring. The First Communion garments were so treasured that it was the norm for a young lady, twelve or more years later, to wear her communion veil as a part of her wedding attire and her first communion dress might be worn by the flower girl. The veil and dress was passed down to several family members until it made its final stop at the wedding of the original wearer. I never doubted but that this tradition of First Communion fashion, as well as all other practices of our local parish was shared by the entire population of Catholics worldwide.

We stood in a line across the front of the altar area. One by one we said those grown up words, "Lord I am not worthy…" and when the priest placed the communion wafer onto our tongue, we became Catholics who could now be forgiven for our sinfulness. Now we could confess to the priest, receive our penance, and then take communion like the millions and billions of fellow believers.

The ceremony ended with the priest handing each child a small book called a Missal. My mother still had the Missal she'd received nearly thirty years before and now I was receiving one that I would keep throughout my life, regardless of where I lived or what I believed. It not only contained all of the prayers that we had learned in class, but also page after page of brightly colored pictures. There were pictures of Jesus, Mary, her husband Saint Joseph, Jesus's cousin Saint John, Mary's cousin Saint Elizabeth, baby cherubs and adult angels. There were two pictures of Heaven and one horribly dreadful drawing of the devil. Fortunately, that sinister 'devil page' was located at the back of the book so you could enjoy the beautiful missal for a nice lone time before coming upon the hideous one.

The devil page showed a greenish brown creature who looked like a lizard with scales and horns, large webbed feet, and long hands with fingernails that needed to be trimmed. It had gigantic wings and a huge mouth. No doubt he had just eaten someone. I was fairly sure that it was not a portion of his tongue I saw hanging out of his mouth but the red blood of some naughty child; one who had probably broken some rule of the church that I had not yet been educated about. I nearly wore that page out going back to it time and again, maybe for the shock value or to see if anything had changed--if the monster was still there.

It required very little imagination to expect that God might remove the drawing as a way of saying, "No! That is not Satan. That is nothing more than a science fiction swamp creature!" Every time my eyes looked at the beast, I wondered how in the world anyone could ever believe that this was an accurate illustration of the devil. In my young mind Satan looked more like a human, and not an ugly or frightening one. Despite what scary movies or books might display, I imagined that if someone actually saw him, he wouldn't be a beast, he'd be someone who looked good enough to be able to fool people into believing that it was okay to do the wrong thing.

I tried to avoid the frightful, nightmarish image as a way of protecting my wild imagination. Had I believed that

Satan was that monster in my Missal, I don't know how I would have gotten to sleep, let alone walked the hallway to the bathroom in the middle of the night. As I grew older I held to the belief that the devil was not some gigantic monster but something or someone who could tempt you to reject God by using charm and popularity combined with a special beauty that was hard to ignore.

I had decided that the enemy of God probably looked like a fancy pirate (cool boots, colorful clothes, lots of chains and heavy jewelry). He probably had sparkling gems and shiny coins, maybe foil-wrapped candy; an enticement that was most likely worthless but so alluring that human beings would want to draw closer for another look and maybe a touch. All in all, it was best not to think about it. It was best not to wonder or to fear that he was some green swamp creature that would jump out at you when you least expected it. I reminded myself of that fact on a regular basis.

🕊 🕊 🕊

Chapter 4

MIRACLE NUMBER TWO

Julie had three books about the saints. They were written for young people and were full of pictures. I had practically memorized each page with its beautiful paintings and photographs. I'd take one home and then borrow it again a few weeks later.

Just holding one of the books in my hands felt like holding something magical or sacred and very special. One of the front covers looked like a stained glass window with jewel tone colors and gold along the edges of each page as if it was a holy book.

I liked to look at the beautiful, long haired Saint Agnes of Bohemia (Prague) who had a very wealthy family but still she enjoyed sewing clothes for the poor. She would also visit people who were sick or dying. I wondered if she would tell them that she was Saint Agnes or if she would just tell them to call her Aggie or something like that. It was in these books that I read about the Saint Theresa who lived in Spain during the days of Christopher Columbus. Another one was called Our Little Saint Teresa of the Roses. In her pictures she was always dressed like a nun. I wondered if her friends treated her different because she was a saint or was she just like everyone else? Okay then, I could be Saint Teresa from the United States of America.

It was Julie's older sister Jana who told us that in order for the Catholic Church to grant you sainthood you must have experienced three miracles during your lifetime. Jana was in Junior High, had already received four sacraments, got a weekly allowance, and had kissed a boy. What more credentials did she need considering she was also a purebred Catholic and a Soldier in Christ's army? To me, Jana was the impressive voice of experience.

When school was out and I'd just finished the third grade, Mom told us kids that our family would be moving to San Diego. I wondered if I would not only be leaving my best friend but also my opportunity to pursue my religious ambition. Were my Holy Orders and eventual sainthood geographically limited to the church where the Saint Joseph miracle took place? Would God come along with me to wherever our family was going? I sure hoped that He would.

On the morning that we climbed into our station wagon and left our home at 123 East Michigan Street, Julie was standing there waving goodbye and smiling as if we'd be getting together to roller skate later that day. Maybe her mother had told her that the Prins family moves every three years. I hoped that her mother didn't say that we would never see each other again until we got to Heaven. Just before I got into the car, Julie handed me an Our Lady of Guadalupe prayer card and a little yellowish-white plastic crucifix. I tucked the card in my pocket and held the cross in my hand as we drove away. From that day onward, whenever we moved to another town, we always left in the wee hours of the morning while everyone in the neighborhood was still sleeping. We would leave before anyone had the chance to say goodbye or to make us realize how hard it is to go, again.

That night while dressing for bed, I decided that I would sleep with the crucifix under my pillow and that I would do this every night so that I would never forget my best friend and our plans to be nun-roommates someday. We'd made a pact to be a part of the same convent, the same parish and although Julie never expressed a desire to be a saint, we intended to be best friends and nun-mates for life.

~~ AND THEN IT HAPPENED ~~

If someone had taken a photograph of my face at the moment of my second miracle, it would have shown my eyes as wide as they could open and my mouth looking as if I had just choked on a communion wafer. I was in shock.

Sharron and Lindy were already in bed. I was the last one to get ready so it was my job to turn out the light and shut the bedroom door. As I maneuvered around the unpacked boxes and walked toward the bottom bunk, I saw something glowing on my pillow. There in the quiet darkness of our bedroom I could see that a soft light was coming from my little cross. I had never seen anything like it; a cool glow, not scary or fiery-hot. The cross was no longer yellowish-white. Glowing, it was very pale lime greenish.

I knelt down on the floor beside the bed and just watched for a while, figuring that it might go out in a second or two. My original plan to sleep with the cross under my pillow was delayed by my fear that this miracle might get turned off if touched. I laid down with my head as close to the cross as possible and tried to stay awake to be sure that I wasn't dreaming.

When morning came the cross was yellowish again. It wasn't glowing. Still, I was filled with excitement as I prepared to tell my family about this brief but amazing miracle. Additionally, I would remind them that this was miracle number two as it appeared that they had long forgotten The Eyes of Saint Joseph incident.

In my quest for sainthood a wonderful benefit existed. God knows that children are not always believed when they voice their enthusiastic account of this or that event and so, just as my first miracle was revealed not only to me but also to Freddie and two of my siblings, such was the case with my second miracle (obviously referred to as The Glowing Cross). You see, nearly every night thereafter, the cross would light up so that I had witnesses to its power. There were a few nights when the cross remained yellowish-white without a glow. This occurred after rainy or cloudy days when there wasn't a lot of daytime sunshine coming in through the bedroom window to provide the energy that God apparently decided the cross needed in order to perform its divine duty.

This second miracle took place during the summer before I would enter the fourth grade. It wasn't until I was in the fifth grade that I saw another plastic glow-in-the-dark item and realized the actual 'science' behind my crucifix:

Peter, who sat next to me at school, gave me a tiny white surf board on a blue plastic necklace cord. He wanted me to wear it as evidence to the rest of the class that he liked me. Later that night when the surf board turned lime green and seemed to be giving off light, I understood the whole glow-in-the-dark thing. For a day or two I felt disappointed and confused. Was it a choice that Heaven or the Catholic Church or maybe God was wanting me to make -- to either be a Saint or be someone's girlfriend? Is that how the whole thing works? I made the decision to keep my distance but act friendly toward Peter and I kept the surf board for future reference. I wrapped it in toilet paper and slid it under my mattress. Once done, I felt confident and reassured. I had convinced myself that the surf board situation had nothing to do with the miracle of The Glowing Cross. When it comes to miracles, there are some things you can't explain, you just know them and there isn't anyone or anything that can change your mind or your heart. I knew the truth. I didn't know why God chose me for these miracles, but I loved Him and I knew He loved me.

At night the cross would glow on my pillow -- my earthly cloud, and I felt close to God, close to Heaven. The surf board had been banished to the dark purgatory between two box spring mattresses and if that didn't ease my mind, I knew that I could always shove it into the depths of hell that was the dusty mess beneath my bed.

🕊 🕊 🕊

Chapter 5

TALKING TO GOD

"God, please turn this water into wine. I'm not asking You to make me rich or cute. I'm asking You to hear my prayer right now, today. Please God. Please turn this water into wine."

The 'water-into-wine' request was made every morning as I took a gulp of water with a bitter tasting grape flavored vitamin. I also prayed the prayer after school as I would stand at the kitchen sink and watch the sun create a prism effect through my jelly jar juice glass. I began praying for wine as a fourth grader and continued with this petition throughout my elementary and junior high school years.

Praying like this was not something you learned in Catechism; as a matter of fact, I was fairly sure that this type of prayer was against the rules. I was old enough to have memorized several Catholic prayers and this was not one of them. I created this prayer as a way to remind God that I was still waiting for miracle number three. I was suggesting the water into wine because it had been done before while Jesus was on earth, so nobody was going to be able to come up with a scientific explanation of why it wouldn't count as a miracle.

What gave me the right to make up my own prayers when the church had already set into place the words that God wanted to hear from His people? If you were afraid, there was the Hail Mary. If you were confused, The Apostle's Creed. Feeling guilty? Say the Act of Contrition. Thankful? The Glory Be. Unsure of what prayer to pray? Say The Our Father. There seemed to be a prayer for most every situation but more and more I found myself wanting to use my own words. Making up my own prayers was not meant to be disrespectful but I cannot deny that in doing so I sometimes felt as if I was rejecting prayers that had been provided by the church. They were already printed in the Missal. Prayer Book prayers had been used for hundreds of years by millions of Catholics and apparently they had worked well enough to go unchanged throughout the ages.

Praying as a Catholic child was not always easy. In addition to the memorized prayers that were expected of us, we had learned about numerous saints whom we could call upon to request certain favors or for assistance in a variety of crises. This was a bit confusing at times and I never really got the feeling that praying to the saints was a requirement of the church. I think it was viewed as an added benefit for Catholics who needed a little extra support when it came to asking for something difficult. When I lost my mother's only pair of scissors, for example, I relied upon the help of the saints in Heaven.

Mother had a pair of scissors that she allowed me to use to make clothes for my paper dolls. I was in the third grade. While fashioning new paper dresses, I was listening to my father as he sang and played his ukulele. I got distracted and somehow misplaced the scissors. When I was not able to find them on my own, I voiced a prayer to Saint Christopher, requesting his help in 'finding a lost item'. Then I called upon Saint Jude who is the patron saint of lost causes. Still, no scissors. So I prayed to The Blessed Virgin Mary for divine help in the event that I should have to be punished for losing the scissors. Suddenly it dawned on me that I may have prayed to the wrong saints! Was it Christopher or was it Saint Anthony who helps us to find lost items? Or was it some other saint whose name starts with the letter C or A? I knew that if I had the right saint, he would hear my prayer and then go talk to the Virgin Mary and she would talk to her son Jesus about my problem. Then Jesus would go to Our Father God. But if Saint Christopher was the wrong guy, he and Saint Jude would probably just talk about the whole thing and I wouldn't get any farther than having two saints in Heaven who just felt sorry for me.

Strange that I would issue my prayers of desperation to the saints and never stop to realize that I ought to go straight to the Source of our help, directly to God as I'd been so bold to do with regard to the water-into-wine prayers.

I faithfully prayed the required traditional prayers but just as often I free styled. Maintaining loyalty to the standard issue petitions would hopefully keep me in the good graces of the church. My personalized prayers were never fancy nor were they very lengthy. I often recited a required Catholic prayer and slipped in a personal request quickly, intentionally, and with an unexplainable sense of excitement as if I knew something that no one else knew; as if it was a secret between myself and God. I hoped that although the priests, the nuns, the catechism and the church might call my prayer behavior deviant, that God heard and still loved me. And so every night as I finished my set of memorized prayers, I tagged the water-into-wine request on to the end of the Our Father. I wondered if I needed to learn how to pray in Latin; maybe that would get God's attention if He was especially busy with other matters.

Surely God was listening but why was it taking so long? The time span between my first and second miracle was approximately one year. Now nearly three years had passed. Where was my miracle number three? It occurred to me that maybe there were some rules to follow of which I was unaware. Maybe there was a rule that I was breaking and in so doing, delaying the miracle process.

My life seemed normal enough; nothing special. I looked and behaved like every other girl I knew who came from a strictly disciplined, close knit family. Just like every other child in the world, in California, or at least on Orange Street where we lived, there was school, friends, home, family, church, daily chores, weekends, birthdays, holidays. My friends wished they could be a princess or a movie star or a famous ballerina or the girlfriend of the guy from Herman's Hermits and their wishes changed every few months. I wished to be Sister Teresa (the nun) and then Saint Teresa of the something or other and I wasn't planning on ever changing my mind. I was wishing to become something that can actually happen in real life, not just in your dream world. I guess I was somewhat different in that I knew what I was going to be when I grew up but I didn't flaunt my incredibly exciting vocational awareness or my ambitions for a glorious destiny. I was a sixth grader now. I knew how to play it cool.

I was described by most as shy or reserved, preferring to be alone in my room, spreading out my collection of prayer cards across the bottom bunk where I slept and memorizing the words on them like some kids did baseball cards. My treasures were the cards, my florescent crucifix, my Missal, and my thoughts. It seemed to me that I experienced a very normal way of being with the exception of Sunday mornings.

When I sat in church each Sunday morning, my mind was absolutely consumed with the pleasant notion of becoming a saint. I would look at the nuns and think, 'that will be me someday'. I would look at the statues of the saints and think, 'someday'. I loved how the nuns wore the same outfit of clothing all of the time: Their long black gown with a crisp white collar, a black fabric veil that covered their hair, came across their shoulders and down to their waist, held in place by a white headband. I even liked their heavy black shoes and socks that looked as if they belonged to someone's dad (which I decided meant something about maybe wearing God's shoes and somehow sort of being His feet here on Earth or something like that). Nuns and saints never had to wonder what they were going to wear tomorrow; that's the kind of life I was looking forward to. These exciting thoughts gave me great joy and were only interrupted by a sometimes harsh awareness, a reminder that miracle number three seemed long overdue.

It crossed my mind that maybe there were already enough Saint Teresas in the world. Not a problem. I was willing to change my name. As a matter of fact, some people do just that when they become a nun or a priest. Mrs. Risso, a friend of my mother, had a sister named Irene who became a nun and was called Sister Mary James when she joined a convent, took her Holy Orders and became a bride of Christ. I didn't have to be Saint Teresa of the U.S.A. I could be Saint Terri or Saint just-about-anybody for that matter. I wasn't fond of the name Ignatius or Bartholomew; otherwise, I hoped that God knew that I was pretty good about changing my name if that's what He needed me to do.

I wondered if when we moved away I had left behind my potential for experiencing miracles. Maybe some little girl whose family had moved into our house on East Michigan Street received the miracle that was intended for me. I wondered if God was privy to anything in particular that I might have been doing that would cause Him to hold out on me or to give my miracle to someone else. Maybe He was ready and willing but was waiting until I got myself under control.

So, what were the rules? The commands? I'd learned about the Ten Commandments way back in the first grade level of Catechism. I memorized and would never forget them but I also remembered that the nuns had said something about the reason that these rules were made. It was because the people at that time were actually doing those things that needed to be written down and called 'against the law in the eyes of God'. I didn't think people did those things nowadays, like coveting, bearing false witness, adultery, taking God's name in vain, killing, and stealing. In my little world people were kind. Children only got into trouble because they were still young and still learning how to become good. I didn't know of any commandment breakers except for the time back in 1963, just months after we'd moved to Sand Diego, when a man committed murder by killing the President.

I was nine years old and it was the worst thing that had ever happened in my life when our President was shot and killed during a parade in Texas. It was my worst day ever because it was the first time I ever saw my mother cry. Everyone got sent home from school in the middle of that day and then it was never discussed again; not in my home, not at school nor at church. When it came on the news, my mother would turn it off except on the Monday that we watched his funeral on television. Mother kept us home from school and I thought everyone else stayed home until my friend Delia asked where I'd been that day. I didn't understand the how and the why of what had happened but I did understand that it was not acceptable for me to ask questions about something so horrible. I lived in a safe and sheltered world where I believed that every church was a Catholic church, every child was a friend of Jesus, and people abided by the rules.

In my quest for sainthood and a third miracle, I reviewed the Commandments again and again until I was certain that although I may have been missing the mark in some other area, I was in compliance where the Thou Shalt Nots were concerned. Still, just to be on the safe side, when I went to Saturday morning confession, I would tell the priest that I was sorry for anything I had done that I couldn't remember about. I even took to apologizing to God when I wasn't in the confessional -- when I was just sitting on the steps of the front porch or walking around the neighborhood looking for heart shaped rocks. I knew what the church taught about that. I knew that only a priest could bring my sins to God and get forgiveness for me. If I wasn't in the church, in the tiny curtained confessional booth, my apologies didn't actually count but I still felt the need to remind God how sorry I was for anything I might have done to offend Him. I didn't want to do anything that might prevent Him from working just one more miracle in my life so that I could hurry up and become one of His saints.

$$\mathcal{Y} \quad \mathcal{Y} \quad \mathcal{Y}$$

Chapter 6

THE NEGRO CAJUN

I was a girl in trouble and now I was old enough to know that my behavior was the reason that it felt as if life was holding its breath until I made right what I was doing wrong. No, I didn't lie or cheat or hate or kill but I had my own methods of defiance.

If I was going to be honestly honest, I had to admit that there were a number of things I did that I would never confess to the priest. I knew about them and God knew about them and they were too wrong to discuss with anyone else. A prime example of my wayward ways was my occasional imaginary friend The Negro Cajun and my prayer life, both of which would certainly have displeased the church and, therefore, might be displeasing to God. You see, not only did I offer up impromptu prayers, I was oftentimes disrespectful of the traditional ones.

One prayer in particular served to occupy my imagination and entertain me during the very solemn Sunday mass. It is called The Act of Contrition and is said by every confessing Catholic in the whole wide world. The words are very serious and they tell God how horribly sorry we are for our sins:

> Oh my God I am heartly sorry for having offended Thee and I detest all my sins because of Thy just punishment but most of all because they offend Thee my God who art all good and deserving of all my love. I firmly resolve with the help of Thy grace to sin no more and to avoid the near occasion of sin. Amen.

Whenever I prayed this prayer, I said it correctly and sincerely. During Sunday mass, however, when the priest would lead the prayer, I used to wrap my arms around my ribs so that I wouldn't laugh out loud. He would come to the part that says, "…to sin no more and to avoid the near occasion of sin", and I would pretend that he had said "…avoid the Negro Cajun of sin." Why I found that so incredibly humorous, I don't know but inside of my head I could see myself falling off the pew where I sat and rolling around in the aisle of the church just giggling out loud.

These thoughts were never of a racist nature mind you; they were so much more innocent than that. I didn't have a clue what the word Cajun meant. I had seen but never actually knew anyone of African-American heritage with the exception of Sidney Poitier whom I secretly adored. In the summer between second and third grade I saw him in a movie where he played the role of a carpenter who loved

God and who was very kind to the Catholic nuns. I loved him for all those reasons.

I had a definite mental image of the Negro Cajun whom we were supposed to avoid. He was tall and had very dark skin, sparkling brown eyes and a huge smile on his face. He was wearing a green, purple, yellow, and black plaid suit jacket with bright orange and red scarves draped around his shoulders. For some reason his gray and brown striped pant legs were rolled up as if he had crossed a river or puddles of water. He looked like a gypsy traveler and could not have been more joyful and friendly in appearance. He played a worn out red and gold colored accordion and had a large tapestry carpetbag full of something or other. Of course the church would want us to avoid him -- he was the very image of adventure and excitement.

There was a dark skinned saint in one of Julie's books. It was Saint Moses of Ethiopia and he had been a bandit-thief back in the 400s. I'm sure that my Negro Cajun idea had not come from the Saint Moses page but I can tell you this for sure: If the Negro Cajun was a saint and there was a statue of him and a miracle occurred while I was looking at the statue -- the miracle would have been that the statue just started to laugh and laugh and laugh like nothing I had ever heard inside the walls of the very serious, never smiling, very 'speak-in-a-whisper' Catholic church. It wouldn't have been naughty or mean or scary laughter; it would have been happiness and joy that just tumbled out of The Negro Cajun's smile. Now *that* would be a miracle worth waiting for!

The Negro Cajun of sin prayer was not the only word play that I enjoyed but it was definitely my favorite. I was also disrespectful in the way in which I said my penance. Following catechism class on Saturdays was weekly confession, a requirement for everyone who intended to take communion at mass on Sunday. In the tiny and dimly-lit booth, I would kneel on a low bench and whisper, "Bless me Father for I have sinned. My last confession was seven days ago." I would confess my sins to the priest whom we always addressed as Father. He would speak to me in a very kind voice and speak to God in Latin. I was sure that God spoke English but that truly important things had to be said to Him in Latin. The priest would then assign the penance prayers determined by how bad you were and how often you were bad. I fully understood that penance is what you do to show that you are truly sorry (heartly sorry) for your sins.

The sins I had to confess were almost always the same: I rolled my eyes when mother was talking to me about something boring (about 5 times), I had bad thoughts about the two girls who live across the street (2 times), I made a mean face at my little brother (one time, maybe two), and I snapped my teeth whenever anyone asked me to do something that I didn't want to do (about 10 or 20 or 30 times). Week after week my penance was two Hail Marys, two Our Fathers, and one Glory Be.

The only time the priest changed my penance was the week that I confessed my brother Richard's sins. I didn't ask him for permission. He'd had a bad week. I thought about all that he'd been in trouble for and I decided that if I confessed, and he confessed, maybe he wouldn't get into so much trouble the following week. Richard's sins were that he couldn't stop smiling when mother was scolding him and when she'd say, "Wipe that smile off your face", he almost laughed out loud (about 3 times), he whistled non-stop when we were supposed to be quiet and then fibbed when he claimed that it wasn't him but the washing machine making all that noise (last Wednesday), and he made up a song with words that were naughty (they had the word "pee" in them). For that penance I had to say The Act of Contrition three times and I am certain that the priest noticed that little Miss Prins had not voiced her normal weekly confession.

After every confession when it was time to say penance, I had a sneaky way to make the time enjoyable, almost fun: To say The Act of Contrition three times for example, I would say, "Oh my God, Oh my God, Oh my God. I am, I am, I am. Heartly, heartly, heartly. Sorry, sorry, sorry", etc. This was not something that I invented. I learned it by watching the older boys and girls saying their penance. Their mouths would move so fast and they would whisper in such a way that it sounded as if they were speaking another language. Praying this way made the whole experience of Saturday morning confession a pleasant time, despite the fact that most everyone around me was very serious and certainly not smiling.

It was not unusual for me to see a few adults doing their penance when I entered the church and still praying when

I was finished and ready to head for home. I had an idea of what that indicated, that they were probably hollerers (you know, those parents who scream at their children). I believed that this was very wrong and that God did not like it one single bit. I thought that if there was another commandment, it should be Thou Shalt Not Yell. These same adults were there each week, kneeling on the padded prayer bar, still praying because they needed to and because they did not know how to do the speedy penance that I took such pride in saying.

How could a little girl who tried to be good have such wild and unacceptable behaviors that would never have been tolerated by any nun or priest and that would probably have gotten me thrown out of a Catholic school had I the privilege to attend? Perhaps it was a good thing that I went to public schools until I could get right and behave like a proper Catholic. Still in all, my greatest rebellion seemed to be my greatest comfort and that was the times when, after having recited the prayers of the church, I would say a few words to God from off the top of my heart. They were words like, "O Jesus, I love you so much" or, "Thank you for taking care of me again today". These were not words that I found in any prayer-book or on any prayer card. They might not be allowed by the church but when I said them, I never felt guilty enough about it to make it a part of my weekly confession.

Where did I learn such rebellion? I am proud to say that it originated with my mother. She was the Catholic rebel, my mentor, my example. Mother saw to it that we said our prayers and that we followed the teachings of the Catholic faith. There were no hollerers in our family; no one raised their voice in her household. We each took our turn at saying grace before meals, "God is great, God is good, let us thank Him for our food, Amen." It was from my mother that I learned about speaking to God in words that are not officially a part of any prayer that you'd find in a prayer book.

At bedtime we always recited the 'Now I Lay Me'. It was a prayer that Mother had taught us, one which I assumed every child throughout the world voiced every night in precisely the same way as did the Prins children. I don't know how old I was when I came to realize that mother had added a few extra lines of her own. I must have seen the original unenhanced version in writing somewhere or other and wondered why there were exactly twenty five words missing. I remember saying the prayer as far back as before I was in kindergarten and I continued to pray it unrevised even through the sixth grade (because as is the case with many Catholic prayers, you sometimes don't actually think about what you are saying, you just know that it is your obligation to pray it and speed is a natural outcome of repetition):

> Now I lay me down to sleep. I pray the Lord my soul to keep. If I should die before I wake, I pray the Lord my soul to take. Dear Jesus, please help me to be good and please take care of Abuelo, Santa Claus and Easter Bunny, and all the ships at sea. Amen.

I said the words so quickly each night that I was never fully aware that I was praying for my grandfather who had died when I was a toddler, for two fictional holiday characters, and for one branch of the United State military to the exclusion of all others.

Yes, Mother was the culprit, the original prayer rebel. I could speak informally though reverently to God with faith in His undivided attention because my mother did so on countless occasions. With six children who were barely one year apart in age, she needed that direct line to God. The closest she ever came to being a hollerer was when she would slightly raise her voice so that God could hear her above the noise we were making. Several times a day she would loudly plead "God give me patience with these kids!" I owe that most primitive Father/Daughter relationship between God and myself to my beloved mother.

🕊 🕊 🕊

Chapter 7

THE NIGHT HAS A
TOUSAND WHYS

Sometimes the news is so devastating that you don't want to know the details; you want to go backwards to the time before you found out. I'd just finished the sixth grade. Summertime began with something that felt like an ugly, too fast first time roller coaster ride downhill in the dark of night without a seatbelt, in the rain.

I had been spending my Saturday afternoons at the library checking out colorfully illustrated books about sainthood, the martyrs, and the life of Christ. Living in a predominantly Catholic region probably contributed to the fact that books about saints and the church were plentiful in the Junior and Teen Section at the public library. In reading the books, I discovered the nearly heart-stopping fact that sainthood is always, *always,* ALWAYS conferred upon an individual posthumously, a fancy Latin way of saying, "after you have died"! I had to believe the words I read because I couldn't prove them to be wrong. I casually asked family members and a few friends about the matter. Not wanting to sound desperately disappointed, I would act as if I'd known all along when everyone gave the same answer, that indeed sainthood comes after death. Good grief! What's the use in that? I wanted the halo and the statues of me while I was living and breathing and I wanted to sit and talk to the people who prayed to me for help with their problems. What's the use in being a celebrity of the church if you're not here on Earth to enjoy the attention? How did I not know about this? I was twelve years old and I prided myself in knowing how to be Catholic. Did my mind wander so much during catechism and mass that I didn't get this bit of earth shattering information? Why would anyone receive miracles in this life only to become a saint once they'd moved off of the earth and into the far-away expanse of Heaven?

I had just graduated from Las Palmas Elementary School. They gave out awards and ribbons and I got one for Best Personality. I certainly hadn't voted for myself because I thought Best Personality meant that you were the most well behaved person in the entire school (and I could not, with a clear conscience, claim that title). I thought it would be cool to get Most Popular but I knew that Mary Ann Paradowski had that in the bag. I never had slumber parties and I didn't twirl the baton at the front of parades so I had to settle for Best Personality. Mother told me later that my award meant that I was "the nicest". With this honorarium, life should have been looking good for me as I approached junior high school and the time when I would finally get to become a soldier in Christ's army by participating in the sacrament of Confirmation. Unfortunately and unexpectedly, the news about becoming a saint *after* you die just sort of put a heavy dark cloud over my heart and it was difficult for me to feel the normal excitement that comes with the beginning of summer.

I had discovered early on that the world is packed full of last minute let-downs, unexpected things that pop up and disappoint, like making wonderful outdoor plans only to wake up to a day full of rain after it being dry for the past two months. Or trying on your summer clothes only to discover that they no longer fit your growing body. A let-down is figuring out the shortest walk from your house to a friend's house and then learning that your family is going to move away so it doesn't really matter if you discovered a shortcut. Or wondering if your smiling aunt is about to tell you how pretty you look but she says "You need to stand up straight and hold your tummy in." Disappointments are like finding a new best friend and then having to move to another town just three years later.

I knew that life has lots of not-so-great surprises but that if you're smart, you know that you'll be okay and that compared to being really sick or something, they aren't that big of a deal. The not-getting-to-be-a-saint-until-I-die shocker was a big deal and it was going to be a lot more difficult to live with. I was going to be okay but it was going to take a lot longer this disappointment-time around. I needed to have something in my life that was certain and it needed to be the thing more important to me than anything else. I needed to be certain about my future, my 'world without end amen' future.

So much of my religious education focused on the things that would keep a person out of Heaven. I didn't like to dwell on the thought of it and I certainly never spoke about it but the matter of hell, hell fire, eternal damnation, the flames in a place called Purgatory, and the souls of 'the lost' was discussed in catechism classes from the time I was a first grader, continuing as I progressed through each grade level of Catholic studies. There were the venial sins that hurt God's feelings and could be forgiven once confessed. And then there were the mortal sins. Those were the God hating/church hating, sometimes unforgiveable sins that when you died, sent you straight to hell unless you were fortunate enough to get to a church, into the confessional, tell the priest about it, be heartly sorry, swear to never do it again, hopefully get absolution, do your penance and be done with it. But what if some unexpected catastrophic event took your life before you could get to a church? What if you were on your way there but got run-over by a car? What if the mortal sin made you too sick to go to confession and even too sick to ask for a priest to perform Xtree Munkshun?

What about people who live on farms where there's no Catholic church nearby? What if the weather is too rough for you to even walk six blocks to the church? What if it was a mortal sin and you thought it was a venial sin! What if you got to the church and the door was locked? Or, how about this: What if the absolutely worst let down in all of creation happened when you thought you were forgiven but then you died and found out that the words the priest was saying in Latin were the wrong ones and even though he did the Xtree Munkshun, you really weren't forgiven at all!

I needed some kind of assurance that I wouldn't spend eternity anywhere but near to God in Heaven. I had already figured out that that kind of assurance comes to the nuns and, obviously, to the saints. The very notion that I might not get to become a saint filled my mind with questions that I couldn't even form into complete thoughts. One thing I knew for sure was that God created everything, so He can change anything that He wants to change. I knew that it would take an incredibly understanding and a very loving God to grant my request and I knew that He was all of those things. And so I said to Him, "Why not let me be a saint throughout eternity in Heaven, but first let me be a living saint for a long, long time before I become a dead one."

Long before I'd even thought about being a saint, I had been taught by the catechism and by my mother (even by Sidney Poitier in the movie) that God loves us all the same. As I grew older and had time to think it over, I decided that maybe they were mistaken. Although no one had ever told me so, I believed that God's very favorite people where obviously the ones that He made into saints and His second favorites were the nuns and priests of the church. I believed that this was very simple to figure out and I couldn't imagine that anyone might argue that I was wrong. It was not my opinion, it was my truth that the main reason I needed to be a saint was so that I could be sure without any doubt that I was one of God's favorites and that I wasn't someone He might forget about. How else could I be sure of having a permanent place in Heaven? How else could I be certain that all of my sins were forgiven unless I knew that I was somewhere near the top of God's list of favorite children? And how does someone get to the top of that list? You become a saint. I liked the idea of being a celebrity in the church but the truly true truth was that I was still a shy type of person who might be uncomfortable if lots of people wanted to be around me. What I wanted was to be a celebrity to God. I wanted Him to think that I was someone very important.

It was looking as if it didn't really matter what I thought or what I wanted; no miracles were happening to me. My big plans for a famous future were beginning to look like a little girl's make-believe life that someone might say I needed to 'grow out of' or to 'get over'.

Why did I want to be a saint? It wasn't actually a matter of wanting something, it was a matter of needing, of absolutely requiring. To say that I wanted sainthood was to minimize its importance. I wanted to wear white go-go boots instead of saddle oxfords. I wanted to rat my hair and wear it in a Molly B ponytail instead of in two braids. I wanted to be allowed to shave my legs before I started Junior High. I wanted to someday own a pair of gold hooped earrings, big ones. I *needed* air to breathe and water to drink and a good night's sleep. And I needed sainthood even more than water or air or rest. I needed to know that Heaven was not a 'maybe' or a 'let's hope so' sort of thing.

I felt certain that sainthood was the key, the nonrefundable, guaranteed ticket to a seat near the Throne of God in Heaven. It was my confidence about these matters that helped me to fall asleep each night and that helped me to smile throughout the days. Despite all that I'd learned, I refused to believe my time here on earth was going to result in punishment rather than reward. I'm pretty sure that it was my assurance in God, in Heaven, in Sainthood, and in being a good Catholic girl that had won me that 6th grade graduation award for Best Personality.

🕊 🕊 🕊

Chapter 8

WHERE WAS GOD?

We lived in Southern California. In San Diego proper, then San Pedro, Long Beach, and then in a few suburbs in San Diego County; always moving to a bigger house in a little bit fancier neighborhood.

Because our family moved to a different town every three years, change was a predictable but always a disruptive part of my young life. Each move involved a different home, a different school, new friends, and a different church. Once relocated, we didn't maintain contact with friends from the past nor did we revisit the places where we'd lived.

You'd think I would figure it out and get used to it after several three year stints but every time mother told us that we'd be moving to another town, the news hit me like it was the first time it had ever happened. No, it was worse than that. The news would hit me in a way that you might expect if you learned that you're not a little girl anymore -- from now on you're a dog or a fish, or the world is actually flat and you're about to be pushed off the edge of it, or it's a law that on your thirteenth birthday if you can't hold your breath for five minutes straight you're going to be put on a big greasy oil tanker ship and sent to live in Siberia without a coat or ear muffs. Hearing that it was time to start packing always felt like the end of the world and I would use up a good two hours, sometime three, getting over the initial shock. After that, it all just sort of worked itself out, no big deal.

Relocating was such a natural part of our growing up that my siblings and I probably benefited more than suffered from each move. We certainly learned how to make friends and to adapt to new surroundings. Perhaps we felt a bit bolder, more comfortable with adventure as we knew that whatever happened, we'd be long gone in a just few short years so it wasn't like we'd establish a reputation or anything. We also didn't establish deep roots and it was always a little sad to hear my mom voice an expression that summed up our lifestyles: "Don't get too attached". Every new home had wonderful fruit trees and flowers and neighbors and a chance to start over fresh and new, if that's the kind of thing you needed to do. Actually, I had been thinking that the next time we moved I was going to try to be a different person, a not-so-shy version of myself.

Some things were consistent: My parents, the loyalty and close knit bond that they required between us kids, and my thoughts about Heaven and sainthood. Those are the things that anchored me to wherever it was that we would call home this time around. When the last of dozens of boxes were packed into the moving van and the station wagon was pulling out of the driveway in the predawn hours of summer, friends, neighbors, playgrounds and classrooms were sadly left behind. Still in all, the things that really mattered were safely stored deep inside of me and kept as close as my imagination wanted them to be.

All that I had learned in catechism, all the things I believed about the greatness of God, and all the plans I had for my future traveled along with me in a place that no bumpy road could jostle. My thoughts required no packing paper, no boxes or suitcases. Best of all, my miracles were as much a part of me as my long braids, my brown-as-a-bean sun tan, and my big family. My two too-wonderful miracles covered every mile that I traveled and caused me to wear a semi-permanent gap-toothed smile.

While relocating provided an early education about change as inevitable, change had an ugly sidekick, an unfriendly companion called Fear of the Unknown. I bargained with God and with myself that as much as I dreaded the confusion of each move, I wouldn't complain or become too afraid of what could be and what might be so long as God would keep on forgiving me for constantly asking Him about the where's and when's and what's of the miracle that would usher me into the society of saints. I refused to give up on Miracle Number Three.

Moving to a neighborhood where the Comacho family had thirteen children whose names you're expected to remember was a challenge but it was do-able. Moving to a house with turquoise walls and fuchsia colored trim was manageable. The 'settling in' obstacles always had a way of disappearing. For me, everything would be okay just as long as God was aware that we'd moved again and just as long as He knew our new address. I wanted to believe that He knew these things. It wasn't enough for me to hope that God came along when we packed up and left, I wanted for Him to arrive before we did and to be waiting for me when I moved in to the next home.

I could always overcome my fretting by filling my mind with imaginary photographs of myself as a nun and thinking about my clever plan to join a convent and stay at least until I was a saint but maybe even longer. It had been a little more than three years since I'd seen my first-ever best friend Julie but I liked to imagine the two of us as nun-mates living in a convent, whispering about this and that while we fiddled with the beads of our rosaries. She would be wearing her rosary around her neck and I'd use mine for a belt to fashionably cinch the waist of my gown. We could talk about the strange and mysterious things we saw just because we were Sister Mary Julie and Sister Mary Teresa or whatever our names were.

I remembered the time when Julie's sister told us about a famous person in some other country who was excommunicated because he fell in love with a woman who wasn't a Catholic. Or maybe it was the other way around, she was Catholic and he wasn't. I don't remember that part but there were romantic details and Jana explained that excommunication means that if you marry someone who isn't Catholic or if you so much as go to a church that isn't Catholic, you can be kicked out of the whole Catholic faith. You don't get to be a Catholic anymore. Jana told us that if you go to a slumber party and they want everybody to go to their church the next day, you have to ask the parents to take you home if their family isn't going to a Catholic church. If you don't, you could be kicked out for good.

I filed this bit of information somewhere in my crowded little mind in the event that it should come up in catechism class on a test or something, or if I might get invited to a slumber party. I was about ten years old when I became aware that other religions exist and, apparently, everyone who was not a Catholic was called a Protestant because they might love God but if you tried to get them to be a Catholic, they would protest. My mental image of excommunication was that of getting a letter in the mail saying that the church has kicked you out but I was convinced that it would feel like you were having your head chopped off by a rusty old guillotine. Not a pleasant thought. Not something I would chose to dwell on. I preferred to think about someone loving someone else so much that their romance got them kicked out of the church and it was easy to imagine that our love, I mean *their* love was so powerful that God stepped in and told the church to change the rules – no more excommunications, and to stop calling people protestants.

Toward the end of the summer after I'd graduated sixth grade, won Best Personality, learned that sainthood is supposed to occur after death, and was readying myself to begin Confirmation classes in catechism, our family moved to another town. There, the nearest Catholic Church was more than five miles away. My dad golfed on Saturdays and Sundays and mother didn't drive.

To the best of my knowledge no one in my new neighborhood was Catholic. None of the kids went to catechism and, except for one home, none of them went to church on Sunday mornings. We all went to public schools. Nobody seemed to know or to care about the Holy Days of Obligation. The family who lived at the end of the block went to church on Thursdays. Another family, just a man and woman whom I never got to meet, dressed in old fashioned clothes and went to church on Wednesdays, Sunday mornings, and Sunday evenings. The only time I ever heard them speak was when they would yell for neighborhood kids to stay out of their yard.

One great thing about this new location was that field trips at school usually meant going to visit a Spanish Mission. Spanish Missions were ancient Catholic churches and convents that were built when priests came to California from the country of Spain. These missions had beautiful flower gardens and stained glass windowed chapels and paintings on walls that depicted life in the olden days. How great it was to live in San Diego, a city that was actually named after Saint James. Many of the cities nearby were named after saints. That just shows how much everyone loves the people who God chooses to be His favorites. I could have spent time thinking about the possibility of someday having a city named after me, but that was almost too big an idea to even consider. I didn't think about things like that except when I'd hear someone talking about the weather in Santa Anna or Santa Clara or Santa Monica or Santa Barbara.

Sundays found most kids on Maynard Street washing their parents' car or sitting in lawn chairs on the driveway listening to Jefferson Airplane or The Doors on the radio while the adults stayed indoors and watched the ball games. Someone would be climbing into a car to head for the beach, or returning at sunset from a long day of surfing and sunning. They skate boarded and built ramps to do daring jumps. When I wasn't body surfing and soaking up the sun at Mission Beach or the Silver Strand, I spent time experimenting with hairstyles and readying my limited wardrobe for school. Religious education was not to be a part of my weekend schedule for this three year segment of life.

Whenever possible, mother made arrangements for us to attend church but these occasions were rare enough that they numbered less than five or six times over the course of three years; Easter Sunday and Christmas. My plans to become Sister Mary Teresa and to eventually be referred to as Saint Teresa (or maybe Our Blessed Saint Teresa of...something or other, I still wasn't sure about that part) remained solid although some clouds of doubt were gathering in my mind. I knew the source of my quandary: I desperately needed to get to church, to be in the presence of God so that He would know that I had not forgotten Him. In church, I could be sure that He wouldn't forget that I had two miracles and was still waiting for milagro numero tres (lots of really cool sounding Spanish speaking in the neighborhood we'd just left but none on Maynard Street). The perfect miracle, one that would help everyone in my neighborhood as well as earn me a halo, would be if someone came to the big empty lot by the shopping center (less than a half mile from my home) and built a Catholic Church.

It seemed to me that if I wanted God to make miracles happen in my life, the least I could do was go to church on Sundays. I had been taught that God is present in the mass. Mass takes place at the church when the priest goes before God on behalf of the people by speaking beautiful sounding words in Latin and then leads us in prayer, speaks about the life of Jesus, and presents the sacrament of communion. Even though the communion wafer is just a wafer and the wine is just grape juice, there were some Latin words that the priest would speak and they had special powers to cause the bread and wine to actually become the flesh and blood of Jesus. It's called transubstantiation; that's practically twenty letters and I don't think there's a word that is as long or as important to people who are real, serious Catholics. Can you understand then how urgent it was for me to attend church and to be in the presence of God and His Son Jesus? How was I supposed to live a normal, everyday life and not go to church?

Month after month the weekends would come and go until Saturdays eventually became a day to sleep late and Sundays were just another day of the week. Can you imagine what the penance would've been had I finally gotten to confession on one of those summer days in 1968 and said, "Bless me Father for I have sinned. My last confession was 116 weeks ago." I had always said "my last confession was seven *days* ago". So now, if I've figured it right, I'd need to say, "my last confession was eight hundred and twelve days ago." I couldn't even bear to think those thoughts. It made no difference if the church was five miles or five hundred miles away, I wasn't there. Every night before I went to sleep I would tell myself that I needed to just keep on praying, and waiting and believing that God does not forget His children, especially the ones that He's got big plans for.

꙳ ꙳ ꙳

Chapter 9

AUTUMN SPLENDOR

In late July of the summer that I was about to enter the ninth grade we traveled to Purcell, Missouri to visit my father's relatives as we had done for many summers past but this time was different. This time we would only return to Maynard Street long enough to pack our boxes, wait for the two Mayflower Moving vans, and say an emotional "goodbye" to our life in California.

We moved to the tiny rural town of Oronogo, Missouri where it appeared that the population was the Prins family and a handful of others. My grandparents lived in the farming town of Purcell and, remote as it was, it differed greatly from Oronogo, just about three miles down the road.

My grandmother told us about our new home town and how it got its name. She said that in the late 1800s people were finding ore in the area and they believed that it could become a very rich mining town if there was enough to be mined and sold throughout the United States. The bankers and investors were taking a big risk in persuading men to uproot their families and move into the town to work in the mines. They knew it was ore or 'no go'. As it turned out, the town quickly came to be known as having the world's largest open-pit led and zinc mine. It was called The Circle Cave Mine. Grandmother said that the town had shopping, an opera house, a fire station, dance hall and saloons. It was considered to be 'the city' by the neighboring farm towns until sometime in the 1940s. Now the city was just homes, the Post Office, and the collapsed mine pit. Now it was 1968. Now it was *our* family who had 'uprooted' for some reason or other and moved to Oronogo, the 'city' that looked nothing like my grandmother's description.

The Circle Cave Mine was still there. It was the size of about a dozen acres of farmland, about the size of four or five city blocks. Now filled with crystal clear water from underground springs, it simply looked like a lake. Tall trees circled the cliffs around the lake. There were lots of rocks that jutted out from the walls of the cliffs and looked like stair steps leading down to the water.

My dad purchased a two story with balcony, full basement, 'picture-on-a-Christmas-card' brick house with an enormous yard and trees that stood taller than the house itself. The upstairs bathroom was the size of our previous living rooms. There was a deep, claw-footed tub and a shower the size of a walk-in closet. With high ceilings, tall beveled windows and hardwood floors, the house had a sort of museum feel. There was a large, screened-in room off of the living room where ladies must have 'taken tea' and looked out at the lilacs once upon a time. No doubt, it was a show case in its day (back when Oronogo had the

Opera House and a Mercantile and hundreds of ore-mining families), but in recent years it had been neglected, needing serious updating. It was a long way from anything we'd ever experienced.

We moved in during a season that my grandparents referred to as 'the dog days of summer' when the humidity is nearly as high as the temperature and the temperature is in the hundreds. Hot and lonely, I could sit in the front yard every day for a week and never see a single person pass by. Mother had taught us that life will go on and "eventually we will settle in" but it was different this time around. We'd gotten older and our friendships were much more difficult to part with. I had learned how to follow my mother's instructions to not get too attached; I'd taught myself to make friends but never so close that anyone feels like family. I knew that with each new friendship came the eventual "goodbye", so I was careful not to have friends that were like Julie back on Michigan Street.

I had grown up in a household full of laughter, practical joking and teasing but now that we were in Missouri, it sort of looked as if that kind of happiness had gotten lost in the move. Maybe things would change once the weather cooled down or once school officially began.

It appeared that I was residing in a one church town. The lady who worked at the post office informed me that the nearest Catholic Church was over the narrow river bridge and across several winding roads that eventually got you in to the city of Webb City, a fifteen minute drive that felt like an hour. I assumed that all the local Catholics knew better and lived in Webb City rather than to mess up their cars by driving on the roads in the antiquated mining town of Oronogo.

We were expected to make a smooth and speedy adjustment from perpetually sunny, predictably 73 degreed ocean side bonfires and sunsets to a landscape of ten foot stacks of mining residual rock fragments called chat piles, deep water filled mining holes, pot-holed asphalt or dirt roads, and a house from the mid-1800s. The things we took for granted did not exist here. Now our back yard didn't have tangerine trees or the lemon, pomegranate, peach, fig, nectarine, plum, and tangelo trees that brought the kids in the neighborhood to our yard. There was no ocean, no skate boarding or lawn chair parties on patios and driveways. Houses were farther apart so the next door neighbor might be 'up the road' or 'across the way'.

We caught the school bus at the Post Office and it transported us to and from Webb City. Richard, Sharron, and I went to the High School, Lindy and Lloyd to the Junior High, and Robby to the sixth grade. Everyone was friendly and we were well received. It was great to discover that our classmates and teachers were not much different than the people we'd spent our days with when we lived 1,600 miles to the west.

September of 1968 passed and October arrived like an enormous, elegantly gift-wrapped package that I was not expecting. I experienced something I had seen in books and magazines but never in California, never in real life.

I was fourteen years old and my eyes were seeing for the first time the true season of autumn.

I woke up one October morning and noticed that the desolate town of Oronogo with its east, west, north and south vistas of gray colored mountains of chat and dusty gravel had been gloriously transformed. Now this little ghost town, this former mining hole was a jewel box of gold, oranges, reds, crimson, purples, and at least a dozen shades of yellow. In whichever direction I turned I could see the variety of colors and every day they changed just a little, getting even more wonderful. Early on I thought I could compare this to an ocean sunset on Coronado Beach but after a long day of blue sky, the California sunsets lasted just fifteen or twenty minutes. This newly discovered beauty was there when I woke up in the morning, throughout the day, and even through the nighttime.

While riding the bus to school, looking out the window at the magnificent trees, it occurred to me that God is present in the beauty of autumn. I reasoned that in some quiet but fantastic way He exists in every single one of the leaves that floated past the window of the bus and formed colorful piles along the roadside. The leaves were like the hands of God waving a greeting to those of us who were aware of His presence. What an incredible experience it would be to witness as He took a jewel box down off of a cloud in Heaven, opened it, spilled its contents across this little section of the world, and called the gift Autumn.

When clouds streaked the sky with pink and lavender against the bluest of blues, God was present -- not above the clouds but right there in the midst of them, probably holding a holy paintbrush in His hand. At the end of every day the sun would prepare to set as God was just beginning the night shift. I had never before seen a harvest moon and now at nighttime when the huge orange-gold sphere lit up the sky, it appeared as if the very face of God was touching the earth, kissing us goodnight and saying "Go ahead, go to sleep. I'll keep an eye on things". I was so excited to discover this aspect of God that I found myself thinking about it on every bumpy bus trip to and from school.

I considered that if Jesus can come into the church, into the communion wafer and wine, why couldn't He also enter into the things of nature? Yes of course, God was definitely present in all of His creation! As much as I loved Him, I loved Him even more for teaching me about these things. I quickly learned to love Oronogo and Missouri and whatever beautiful surprises might be coming next. I reasoned that people waste their time wondering where God is and always looking for Him when, in fact, He never moves -- it's us who move. We imagine that we have lost sight of Him when He is right there, right here where He's been since we first opened our eyes. I began listening for His voice in the music I heard. In the autumn breeze I imagined that He brushed my face with His hand and that sometimes I was actually feeling the very breath of God.

I didn't feel like a little girl anymore. I had discovered a new, beautiful, romantic way of looking at life. Yes, I had discovered romance (and how could I help it, considering the things we were reading in English Literature class?). So this is what the songs were talking about! And, as life would have it, I discovered an exciting new way to look at and think about boys. I made a conscious effort to keep my discovery pure and holy by diverting my delicious thoughts away from the venial sin called 'lust of the flesh' (or, I wondered, is lust a mortal sin and is there a saint I should pray to about this?). Instead, I pointed my overflowing young heart toward Heaven, toward my faith in God, and toward the exciting future that I was still pretty sure He had for me.

I tried out and got a part in the theatre department's production of a play called Bobby Sox. I went to rehearsals, memorized my lines and did a good enough job to get lots of attention and lots of applause. In doing so, however, I discovered that I did not want to be an actress or a celebrity or a famous anything. I didn't want to 'wow the crowd' and I actually preferred life on a smaller scale than on a stage in front of a cheering audience. I'd had these same feelings while attending school sporting events and pep rallies. Apparently, the shy side of my personality hadn't disappeared just because I'd moved to a new town.

All of this seemed to inform me that the fame and attention I was seeking by becoming a celebrity of the church as a saint was perhaps not what I really needed or wanted after all. Ah ha! No wonder people don't become saints until after death! No wonder they get their statues and pictures and prayer cards made after they have moved upward to Heaven! The fame comes once they're at peace and away from the crowds and the noise. I was glad to learn that these things had become less important to me. Now I could view sainthood more realistically. Now I would think of sainthood as being remembered after you die as one of God's favorite people in the whole wide world.

This approach to everyday life severed me well, offering me joyful excitement and making me sensitive to everything around me as if I awoke to a new world every morning. While life was introducing me to a variety of first-time emotions, I found myself struggling a bit with what I guess would be called restlessness. I was a good Catholic girl, hopefully one of God's favorite daughters and so I was ready for Him to provide me with a boyfriend. Compared to many of my classmates, I was a late bloomer for sure but now I was ready and waiting for love or at least for a guy friend or maybe just a first date, one little kiss, some hand holding, something, anything. I would be selective without coming across as overly picky. On second thought, maybe to make up for lost time I would limit my choice to anyone who had both x and y chromosomes and was nice enough come my way. It would be great if he was tall and it would be great if he wasn't as shy as me and maybe if he was also on the basketball team.

My birthday was still a few months away but I made a plan that when December twenty second came around I would do something I'd never done before. Birthdays in the Prins house were always the same: homemade two layer cake, the correct number of candles, the birthday song, the wish, then the second verse of the birthday song: "God is blessing you now, God is blessing you now..." But this year, after always making same silent wish that I could be a saint and never go to hell, the wish would be different. My fifteen year old birthday wish was going to be for a kiss. For kisses. For a boy to gift me with hand holding and kisses and phone calls and kisses and love notes and kisses.

🕊 🕊 🕊

Chapter 10

KISS THE CONVENT GOODBYE

It seemed as if there'd never been a time when I wasn't making plans to someday become a nun and a saint. I'd even considered joining an order where the sisters took a vow of silence and spent their days not teaching or being nurses but in prayer for hours at a time. They prayed for the entire world; now that's an impressive career choice. Suddenly, however, after nearly seven years of planning, the convent was no longer on my agenda. Nunnery or Sisterhood would no longer be my vocation.

It happened early in the first semester during my freshman year at Webb City High School. I was the reluctant third wheel on my sister's date with her boyfriend to a school dance. There, while standing in a cluster of girlfriends, a tall smiling redheaded boy who played on the basketball team walked up and asked me to dance. He not only danced his way into my evening, he sealed the deal by giving me a good night kiss that was better than anything I'd ever imagined. It wasn't one of those kisses that happen at a spin-the-bottle party. This was the kind of kiss that doesn't go away; it lingers for a few days, then weeks, then months after the fact. It was the kind of kiss that, could it have been bottled and used as a drug, was so potent it could have healed the sick and would have made an addict of a weaker girl.

The dance had ended and my partner walked me to the car where I was to wait for my sister and her boyfriend. Maybe the fact that the kiss was unexpected contributed to the pleasure. Whatever it was, I knew that I didn't know how to kiss back so I just sort of stood there. Fortunately, I'd seen some kissing in the movies so I was at least savvy enough to keep my mouth and my eyes closed and to sort of move my head back and forth, side to side just a little bit. The crisp nighttime breeze went unnoticed for a moment as my face, my hands, my whole body warmed up to the thrill of being kissed by this Missouri country boy.

I heard my sister's voice, opened my eyes, and saw that the object of my newly initiated affection, however fleeting, was walking away. No, I was not in love. I didn't give much thought to whether I would see the boy again because I just sort of knew that in a school this small, I was bound to pass him in the hall or maybe have a class with him one of these days. He'd told me his first name but not his last. I wasn't even sure what grade he was in. What I did know for sure was that I would definitely require another kiss. Maybe he would be involved next time or maybe not, but somebody was going to have to give me another lesson in what was now my favorite subject. I hoped it would be soon.

Minutes later as the car pulled out of the school parking lot, a laughing little voice inside of my mind said, "You don't get kisses like that in the convent!". I knew myself well enough to recognize the voice as my own. Just as suddenly, I knew that there had been a radical change in plans. God willing, I would eventually enter Heaven as Saint Teresa of the something or other, but I would not be clothed in the flowing garb of a nun. The convent was out, sainthood was still in, and I needed to cautiously investigate the possibility of finding a library book that gives information on perfecting the art of kissing.

It is a comfort to be able to honestly declare that I did not give myself physically to the boys I dated and that many years later my virginity went to the man I married. I can only make that claim, however, if you don't count kissing as a disqualifier. I insisted that the guys keep their hands to themselves and I gave away kisses as rewards for their abiding by my rules. It didn't hurt that my brothers were on the football team as I think guys knew better than to do something that might get them tackled.

Despite being geographically separated from the church, I felt closer to God than ever as if I had a personal, secretive relationship that the church had probably never heard of and might never allow. I began to reason that a life with God was very simple but that people made it hard. I wanted to believe that everything in life was created to be simple, that nothing was ever intended to be so confusing that anyone could be disqualified or made to feel like a failure. Mathematics, of course, was the exception.

Math was so difficult that I was convinced that it was not something God created. It was probably something that some genius-type invented because he was bored and they didn't have boy-girl dances in his town. I found no beauty in mathematics. Numbers were not things you could hold in your hands. You couldn't feel a number. Numbers were ideas that someone decided was the truth and most of us know that it's impossible for the average person to prove them right or wrong. Mathematics was full of rules and laws that you needed to memorize in order to be successful. It was the very definition of confusing. Numbers and math only made people aware of how complicated life can be. Mathematics made people feel incompetent. Obviously I was having trouble in Freshman Algebra.

I began to see Catholicism as similar to mathematics in that it had a vital place in the world and in each individual life but it was difficult and weighty, sometimes so difficult that the word 'burdensome' would come to mind. Being Catholic was a huge part of my life; it defined who I was and yet I couldn't get my hands around it, nor my heart, nor my brain. I couldn't get a good enough grip to feel secure. Now that my life's vocation did not include becoming a nun, my desire for sainthood intensified (as if that was possible). I was fairly certain that my negative feelings about the church were due to the fact that too much time had passed since I'd sat among the pastel painted statues, the beautiful stained glass windows, and the consistency of the mass that I loved so dearly.

I wasn't good at math but I knew this for a fact: I was 8 years old when I received my first miracle. I was now 14 and that equals 6 years ago. Miracle #2 came in 1962 and now it was coming to the end of 1968 which equates to a total of 6 years without a miracle. I wanted to know for sure that I was going to be a saint so something needed to happen soon. If some investor whose family became rich during the mining days would come back into town and build an Ore or No Go Catholic Church, I might be able to consider that miracle number three. Life would be so much better for me and for all the people who'd go to the same church as had Saint Teresa of the U.S.A.

🕊 🕊 🕊

Chapter 11

UNOFFICIAL EXCOMMUNICANT

I had enjoyed having a locker all to myself but it became necessary to share the crowded space when Merlyna transferred into our ninth grade class.

I had just finished first hour and was walking down the hall when I saw a man and woman standing in front of my locker. I don't know where Merlyna was at the time but her smiling parents were there to shake my hand and to introduce themselves.

They called themselves Brother and Sister Robison. With the exception of nuns and priests, I had never referred to adults in any other way than Mister or Missus and the Robisons were wearing regular-people clothes (plus they had a daughter), so they couldn't have been Holy Ordered. This was something new to me and I assumed it was a Missouri thing that wasn't done in California.

As Merlyna and I became friends, not many weeks passed before I was spending time in her home, eventually sleeping over on weekends, and attending her family's church. Her father was the preacher of the little church that was located next door to their house. It would be impossible for him to drive me home on a Sunday morning because he had to prepare for Sunday services. I had told him that I was a Catholic and still he invited me to attend their church, which brought to mind the words of my friend Julie's sister when she talked about excommunication. I had no means of transportation and so I reluctantly walked along side of Merlyna and her sisters Gloria and Robin on the day that I attended what I thought of as my first non-Catholic mass.

As we entered the vestibule (but they called it the foyer), Brother Robison introduced me to a man named Ivan Simmers. Included in the introduction was a statement that spun my brain around even faster than the big kiss had done just a few weeks prior. After saying Mr. Simmer's name, Brother Robison added, "He is a saint of the church." Whoa! I had never met a saint in person! I'd never touched one unless it was made of plaster. I never shook hands with a saint and I certainly never expected to meet one in a church that had no giant crucifix, no holy water in the foyer, didn't smell like incense, and had not one single statue. As I noticed how brightly lit the sanctuary was, I made a mental note that Ivan Simmers did not have a halo-like-glow around his head and he didn't give off a kind of sainty vibe.

Mister Ivan Simmers had a very kind face, a welcoming smile, and a firm hand shake. I guessed that he was my grandparent's age, maybe a little younger. He resembled what I imagined an elderly Abraham Lincoln would have looked like. I noticed that although he was introduced as a saint of the church, he was referred to as 'Brother Simmers' by everyone who passed by to say "good morning". Oh dear! I might be willing to try new things and to accept changes in this world, but this was something that I would be unlikely to agree to when I was awarded the title of Saint. I was not about to be called Sister Prins or Miss Prins. I would be Saint somebody. I had spent so many years looking forward to being addressed as Saint Teresa (of the something or other). Nope, there was no compromising on the saint word.

Walking into the sanctuary I thought how the title 'Saint Ivan' had a beautiful, musical sound to it. Who wouldn't love to be referred to as Saint Ivan? That Sunday was a good day, particularly because I had met someone who was referred to as a saint and that person was still alive!

It was just a few minutes into the church service when I realized that I was not attending a mass and that I was a long, long way from Mary Star of the Sea and the other parishes of my childhood. There was no golden altar, no candles or Stations of the Cross, no statues to adore. Brother Robison wore street clothes and when he spoke to us from the podium at what was the altar area of the church, he seemed very concerned that everyone understood what he was saying as opposed to expecting us to have learned enough to follow along. What were we supposed to focus on during church? Were we expected to keep our attention straight ahead on him? I liked his voice and the very kind way that he spoke but it was all a bit too much like normal life, a bit too comfortable to be *Church*. Wasn't anything mysterious going to happen to arouse my curiosity and satisfy my bent toward the mystical? I needed for there to be things I didn't understand so that I could use my imagination and my humor to figure them out in a way that would make me want to come back another Sunday.

The church service turned out to be about as far from a Catholic mass as an Oronogo chat pile is from a San Diego sand dune. It looked as if there weren't more than about sixty or seventy people in attendance and they actually appeared to be happy to be there as if they were volunteer church goers. Even the young people walked in as opposed to dragging themselves down the aisle at the very last minute and plopping themselves down onto a pew. Here, people greeted each other with handshakes and hugs and you would have thought they hadn't seen each other in years. This wasn't a mass but it sure was friendly and that made it a new kind of fun for me. I could just imagine the nuns saying, "Teresa! You ought to be ashamed of yourself." But instead of feeling shame I felt such welcome and genuine delight to be among the people who had come to church on that Sunday morning.

Midway into the church service Brother Robison asked if there were any testimonies. Testimonies? I wondered if that was some kind of Missouri thing or a play on words or maybe something scary. This wasn't a court of law but maybe it was about to become one. Maybe this church had some kind of a judgment day thing that they did on Sundays. Maybe that's why everybody smiled a lot and were on their best behavior – because there was going to be testimonies and judgments! I was somewhat familiar with testimonies from occasionally watching Perry Mason on television and then there was the show that Mother used to be watching when I came in from school during the first and second grade. I called it The Vur Dick Kuh Jurs (I didn't have a hearing problem, just a wild imagination); it was actually The Verdict Is Yours.

Testimony time began as one by one the people at Merlyna's church stood to their feet and reported on what was going on in their life. Some folks were upset about problems they were having and some talked about their aches and pains. What all of these reports had in common was their description of how God was helping them to take care of everything.

Most confounding to me was when Brother Robison referred to one particular testifier as "a saint of God". She was an average looking woman around the age of my mother with nothing outstanding about her appearance or her testimony. She was pleasant enough but there was no visible halo and she certainly didn't glow. I was so caught up in the idea that she'd been referred to as a saint, I don't think I actually heard the details of her report. There must have been about eight or ten testimonial reports on that particular Sunday morning. Throughout the testimonies no one appeared bored or disinterested or wiggling around getting ready to go home. Even if what someone had to say was just a bunch of whimpering and crying to where you couldn't understand a word of it, the people sitting around the testifier all smiled and sort of gave off a feeling as if they were saying, "We understand. We know how it is.

Don't worry, we're here for you and God is here for you."
Everyone seemed to be genuinely listening and genuinely
caring. This shouldn't have seemed unusual but it felt very
new because it actually was a first-time experience in my
life. Just when I wondered if this would go on for the next
couple of hours, Brother Robison said, "One more testimony
before we prepare for the invitation." Invitation? To what?

It's funny how we use words expecting that everyone
knows what we're talking about. Throughout his preaching,
Brother Robison kept making sure that everyone was
following along but after the sermon, he tossed out words
such as testimony, invitation, altar call, tithes (and there
was much more to come in future weeks: terms like
sanctification, prayer meeting, revival, world missions).
Especially funny to me on that first visit to their world of
worship was when he told us, "and now Brother Dan has
a special." What on earth was a special? A man named
Danny Burke went to the front of the church and sang "On
the Wings of a Dove". Instantly, I understood what a special
was and why they called it by that name. I had never been
in church when someone sang a solo. It *was* special, very
special. It required only a few return visits to that little
Church of the Nazarene before I was able to make sense
of their unique language. At the same time, the Robison
family patiently endured my questions and my confusion
about their way of loving God.

🕊 🕊 🕊

Chapter 12

SAINT TERESA THE THIEF

I didn't steal from a store. I didn't rob a bank. It was worse, much worse than that. I stole from a Church.

If someone had asked me to use one word to describe my life as a fourteen year old living in Southwest Missouri and seeming to love just about everything around me, I would have used the word that Julie and I invented so many years ago: Sainty. That said it all. It meant that my experiences were Heavenly, sometimes beyond description and that whomever wrote the English dictionary had not come up with a word to describe how wonderful it was to be a Catholic girl who would someday be a saint. Then, if someone looked me right in the eyes and told me to "get real" (a trendy expression that I didn't like), I would have said that the one word which best described my religious experience at this time was Fear. I wasn't sure if it was something that I inflicted upon myself or how much the church/teachers/clergy contributed to my shaky belief system. What I knew was that I had matured into a fear-filled girl when it came to the concept of being religious, of being Catholic. By that time I was what was viewed as a lapsed Catholic because if you don't attend mass on Sundays, you've lapsed into a world of trouble in the eyes of the church and possibly in the eyes of God.

I was not afraid of life in general and I wasn't afraid of God but when it came to religion, I lived with a constant fear. It never intensified or diminished under varying circumstances, it just existed as a big, ugly sensation in response to thoughts about my future, about my destiny. I began to feel that maybe I'd never truly been forgiven of the day-to-day sinfulness that I used to confess to the priest on Saturdays. I began to feel suspicious that there was something important that someone had failed to teach me and that not knowing was going to be my downfall into some flaming furnace call Purgatory (if there was a glimmer of hope for my lost soul) or Hell (if I was permanently doomed). I had not studied for nor received the sacrament of Confirmation – the sacrament that is meant to take away all of your doubts about whose side you're on. Still, I loved my Catholic upbringing and I loved my expectations of the future as a Catholic regardless of the fact that I had chosen against becoming a nun in favor of becoming a girlfriend.

Life was not miserable for me. It was actually better than I'd expected. The only part of my life that was miserable was the religious part. I believed that my love of God was stronger than it had ever been, but when it came to religion and eternity, I felt as if I was living on shaky ground. If it is possible for a teenage girl to be enthusiastically optimistic and miserable at the same time – that was me in a nutshell.

I enjoyed thinking about the Robison's church. I really liked it when Brother Robison would refer to the Bible as "God's Word" or he would call it "The Word of God". Those words always caught my attention because they sounded incredibly powerful and holy. Merlyna's dad preached about the Christian way of life and that it simply involved accepting, believing, confessing, and then living as if you'd done those things and planned to do them from now on. I was sure that it had to be harder than that. There must be something more, something hidden that you'd have to do to be sure of where you stand with God. It just couldn't be as simple as honestly believing, confessing your sins, and then claiming to be His (they called it being "saved"). Brother Robison and the people at his church all seemed to be confident when they testified about knowing that they were going to Heaven someday. They didn't seem like they were confused or like they were faking at all.

And then there were the testimonies. Some actually sounded like miracles. I mean, when someone is really sick and then they're healed -- when the doctors found definite problems and then the x-rays show that the problems are gone, that is a miracle. God was doing miracles in these people's lives and they acted as if they weren't surprised. They were always very thankful and at the same time they seemed to expect them to happen. Miracles were happening in *their* lives but here I was, still waiting for mine.

One afternoon during my last hour class at school I made a list of the things that I had learned while attending catechism and mass. I wrote them on the inside cover of my algebra notebook. The list was entitled

This Is What I Know For Sure

REVERANCE for God and respect for everything and everyone He created. When you reverence God, there is no hate in your life.

MEDITATION instead of medication. You won't ever be an alcoholic or a druggie if you know how to be quiet and listen in case God wants to speak.

SERVICE. Finding out what God wants you to do and then doing it. Doing things that please God. Helping others is helping God.

ACCOUNTABILITY. When you sin, you have to tell a priest about it.

THE CRISIS ON THE CROSS. What happened and why.

I had been a good student of the catechism but that was almost four years in the past. Now I was a straight A student in Language Arts. I liked how certain words sounded when spoken. I liked the clever way that some words looked in print. I wanted to read anything and everything. I loved to write and I enjoyed creating lists. If I'd been more precise in my self-imposed assignment on that particular day, however, I would have added to my list of This Is What I Know For Sure an item number six: FEAR. Fear of never being good enough to enjoy the things I'd learned.

I had a lot to think about. Boys, my Catholic faith, keeping my grades up, my family, boys, becoming a saint, learning more about the Robison's church, and did I say boys? I constantly felt as if I was on the verge of something and I feared that it was a change even too big for me to accept or to easily 'settle-in' (as mother would say whenever we relocated).

Although they consumed a lot of my thoughts, school, family, and boys were not a problem. Those things just sort of fell into place naturally and smoothly. Even kissing had become comfortable and nonthreatening (nonthreatening as in nothing that I would have to confess about to a priest). My concerns were of a spiritual nature. I had the most ominous, most dreadful suspicion that I had lost out on my opportunity to ever receive another miracle or to fulfill my life's ambition to become a saint. I didn't want to give up but I sensed that it was about to become necessary because I had committed what I believed to be a mortal sin.

I took something that did not belong to me. I stole. I was a thief. I knew it was wrong and I chose to do it anyway. I knew the consequence of my action was likely to be separation from the church but I did it and I did it in broad daylight – in broad church light to be exact. Yep, I committed my big sin right there at the Robison's church and it wasn't just some little item that I stole. I stole the Word of God. I stole a Bible.

It happened because they had something that I didn't have and I wanted one. It's not that I felt the need to fit in with them; I knew I was different. I was Catholic and they were something else. I was comfortable with whatever differences existed between myself and this group of people who called themselves Christians. But I really wanted a Bible. I never took the time to consider any other means of obtaining one but through the opportunity that presented itself. I had a clear-cut opportunity for thievery.

During the first few times that I attended their church, I noticed that nearly everyone, including the children, carried Bibles. Most of the Bibles had black leather covers but some of them were red or burgundy colored. Even the children carried pink or white or baby blue Bibles of varying sizes. There appeared to be a trend among the ladies of the church to carry their Bibles inside of flowered calico purse-like pouches.

I had never so much as touched a Bible but I knew it to be The Word of God, thus very valuable and I knew it to be full of important information. I recalled that the priest would read a few sentences of verse from the Bible at each Sunday morning mass. I doubt that anyone dared to wonder why he was the only one who enjoyed this privilege. It was just another one of the mysteries of the church. We had our own prayer book missals which contained condensed reports about certain events in the life of Christ and most churches provided song books for use during mass; otherwise that was all we needed.

I know that times have changed and lay people now enjoy reading and owning their own personal Bible, but during my youth I never once saw a fellow Catholic of any age carrying or reading from one. I never spotted a Bible in the homes of my friends. I know without a doubt that if Julie or her sister Jana had owned a Bible, they would have shown it to me, especially if it had pictures. They would have known that I would want to borrow it.

Getting back to the crime report of The Big Sin: We had just finished the Sunday School session during which time the teacher, Ann, had casually taken a Bible down from a book shelf and handed it to me. On the shelf were several Bibles, old song books, and paperbacks that she referred to as Missionary Readers. Before she handed it to me, Ann opened the Bible to the page where each of us would take a turn at reading a few lines of scripture. Everyone else in the class had their own Bible. I noticed that no one showed any reaction to Ann 'giving me' the Bible.

I was in the class for ninth and tenth graders. Sunday School was an hour long and was held before the church service which they referred to as Worship Service. I liked the sound of that – worship and service. It sounded better than the word 'mass'. I didn't know what the word 'mass' meant for sure but 'worship service' described exactly what happened in the Robison's church whenever I was fortunate enough to visit.

No one called the teacher Sister Ann or Miss or Missus. All the kids called her by her first name even though she was an adult and the mother of five children. Being allowed to refer to a grown-up so informally was enough of a first time experience to occupy my thoughts for the rest of the week. It crossed my mind that it might be a sin to disrespect an adult by addressing her so casually but I really didn't have time to dwell on those thoughts. Why? Because I was sitting in a classroom holding a Bible, The Word of God in my hands! I was looking at what I thought only priests were allowed to read. I was about to read aloud from a Bible! I felt as if I was like one of those pioneers in some new expanse of uncharted territory – a place that was familiar to my Sunday School classmates but new to me. I didn't even think about trying to look cool or sound cool or any of that.

When we stood to leave the classroom and proceed into the sanctuary for worship service, I intentionally held onto the Bible and carried it into the church as if it were my own. It was well worn with raggedy corners. A name was written on the inside cover. Certain portions of scripture had been underlined with an ink pen. While Brother Robison was probably preaching about honesty, truthfulness, and respect for the property of others, I sat beside Merlyna and began reading the first chapter in the first book of the Bible and as I read, my whole being was making plans to go home and read everything that someone had deemed underline-worthy. I wanted to read every word in this Holy Bible. Suffice it to say, this was a big day in my little life.

When church was over and we returned to the Robison's home for lunch, I went into Merlyna's bedroom and set the Bible on top of my overnight case. I set it in plain view and acted as if it was mine; as if I had a right to another person's property. I didn't care that it had someone else's name in it. I didn't wonder if that person had attended church on that particular Sunday or if he was someone I'd heard give a testimony (I did know that I'd never heard a testimony about anyone misplacing their Bible and I'd never heard anyone testify that their Bible had been stolen). I did not give even one second's thought to returning it, nor did I give any thought to how someone might feel when they realized that their Bible was missing. These actions were a million, trillion, zillion miles away from my true character but somehow they didn't feel foreign to me. I had become someone that I'd never known in the past fourteen years of life and it was kind of exciting.

My imagination was not willing to come up with a scenario of what I would have said had someone seen me in the act of intentional, sinful thievery. I refused to imagine what I would have said if asked for an explanation or if, God forbid, I'd been asked to give the Bible back to Ann. I felt sneaky and somewhat ashamed but those feelings were miniscule as compared to the overwhelming thrill I felt at the thought that I now had a Bible. It was as if I suddenly possessed a ring full of keys that would unlock every door that I had tried to open in an attempt to escape from the fear that had defined my spiritual life to that point in time.

Thereafter, each time I spent the night with Merlyna and attended Sunday School and Worship Service, I had the nerve to carry that Bible along with me as if it were my own, never stopping to wonder if its owner might be wanting it back. I never worried that someone might ask

"Where'd you get the Bible?" My reply would have been that Ann "gave it to me". So there I was, not just a thief but a lying thief in the body of a future saint; that is, if my miracle number three could be the forgiveness of this mortal sin.

🕊 🕊 🕊

Chapter 13

CRUCIFIXION CONFUSION

From time to time our high school newspaper would have an article where students had been asked to tell their favorite things or their pet peeves. The answers were typical: favorites were always The Beatles or The Rolling Stones and everyone hated war, speed limits, and loved peace. Pet peeves were usually gossip or bad breath.

I always agreed with the articles but I had a pet peeve that was so much more troublesome, so much more difficult to endure. I would never have admitted to it if interviewed by someone from the Journalism Class. I liked most everything in life and if I didn't like it, I sort of figured that it meant I did not yet understand it.

If asked, I would probably have chimed in with the others and said something like, "I love Paul McCartney and I can't stand that we don't have enough time to get to our locker, the restroom, and then to class without being tardy. In truth my pet peeve, the thing that absolutely unnerved me, was seeing anybody wearing a crucifix as a necklace or a charm bracelet. I detested any depiction of Jesus hanging on a cross looking as if He was either dying or was already dead. I could not fathom why anyone would want to own a piece of jewelry with a crucifix. I didn't care whether it was gold or silver or studded with diamonds, it was terribly offensive to me.

Because crucifixes were such popular items of jewelry, I felt certain that this was my own special problem and that most everyone else was clear on the subject but that I had somehow missed the point. I wondered if I would eventually get over my dislike for crucifix jewelry once I learned about the purpose of wearing a constant reminder of the most horrific thing that ever happened in the history of mankind. If the worst thing that ever happened in the history of *my* life time was the president getting shot, and if everyone loved John Kennedy as much as my family, my friends, my church, my section of the world loved him, then why wasn't there some kind of President's Assassination jewelry like a convertible car on a chain or something like that? We'd been studying the Holocaust. Why wasn't there horrible looking jewelry to wear if you hated what happened and wanted to lovingly remember the people who died such tragic deaths?

Here was my take on it: When I was a little girl in catechism class, I learned about the birth of Jesus. I learned about the Blessed Virgin Mary and the wonderful events that led up to her becoming the Mother of Christ. The details of His birth in the manger, the bright star overhead and the three kings from afar – all of this was so sweet, so wonderful and exciting. The story invited us to imagine ourselves there in Bethlehem kneeling beside this tiny baby who didn't even know it yet, but *we* knew, that one day He would grow up to be the King of Heaven. How could any little Catholic girl keep from falling in love with the Christ Child?

Once we reached the third grade we began learning about the childhood of Jesus, how He obeyed His parents and how He helped His father in the carpenter shop. He had been a little baby and now He was growing up just as we were. What child would not want to please the Lord by imitating His good behavior?

We were invited to become best friends with Jesus and we were always told that Jesus loves us. We learned simple songs about it. There were always pictures to go along with the stories. We saw pictures of Jesus sitting on a big rock in a field of flowers, flocked by little children. They sat on His lap and He seemed to be calling to the other children to come near, to gather around Him. There was the picture of the little boy who gave his lunch to Jesus in the story of the miracle of the loaves and fishes. There was the picture of the little girl that Jesus brought back to life. It was great to know that even though some adults might not like children, Jesus liked them for sure.

By the time we had learned about His growing up, His ministry, His twelve disciples and all the miracles, we were so familiar with Jesus that there was no question that we were privileged to know Him. He was our Friend, our Lord, our Elder Brother, and our Savior all rolled into one.

Believing the stories about Jesus and accepting the details of His life wasn't a matter of faith for this little

Catholic girl. Faith meant believing in things that other people might need proof in order to accept. No, there was absolutely no question in my mind about the reality of Jesus. For me Jesus Christ was a matter of unquestionable fact. Who wouldn't believe? It didn't seem to be a choice to believe or not to believe, it seemed more a matter of whether or not you'd heard the great news about Jesus, the Son of God.

But then things got bad. When I was barely eleven years old Jesus was killed. He was tortured right in front of His friends. He was stripped of His clothing, pushed around, spit upon and humiliated. He was whipped until His back was just shreds of skin. Then they took huge metal nails and hammered them right through the skin in the palms of His hands to attach Him to a wooden cross. Sister Mary Francis told us that Jesus was crying when He was on the cross. And there was more, much more – details too unbearable to even think about.

He had been so strong and beautiful and then He was broken and hard to even recognize because of all the blood, and dirt, and the violence done to His body. This was *my* Jesus that they had killed! This was the Baby in the manger, the little boy who worried His parents when He ran off to go to the temple one day. This was my best friend, the One who could make a storm suddenly stop, who didn't mind spending time with people who had diseases like leprosy.

No! I was way too young to have such a horrible thing happen to someone so important to my life. I was only in the fifth grade and although I knew that what the nun was teaching was true, I couldn't bear to even think about it. At the same time I wanted to know more, to hopefully learn enough to catch Sister Mary Francis in a mistake that would prove her wrong, to prove that it didn't really happen that way.

Of course I knew that this lesson was historical, that it had occurred over a thousand years ago. Still, when you are as immersed in the life of Christ as we had been taught to be, it was as if His death occurred at the very moment I first learned about it. I had always heard references made to Jesus dying on the cross but I ignored them in favor of thinking of more pleasant things. I was probably too immature to pursue the rest of the story. When the death of Jesus became required study in catechism, I had learned enough background information for the morbid account to make sense whether or not I was emotionally prepared.

I had learned from the very beginning of Catholic conditioning that His death provided for the forgiveness of sins but if I ever took a second to think about it any further, I imagined that He had died of natural causes. The tortuous details of His death were minute by comparison to the notion that it happened because of the horrible, rotten defiance of mankind, of womankind, because of my family, because of my friends, because of me. How in the world would I ever come to grips with that?

I knew people who had somehow 'made it through' and 'gone on' to have a happy life after a grandparent had died. I knew of a couple of families who seemed to be okay even though their brothers had been killed in Vietnam. I knew that these people never forget what happened, they just try to focus on other things and try not to let their mind return to that terrible day when they learned the horrible news and their world crashed in all around them. I was somehow able to accept Jesus' death by learning to manage my thoughts so that I wouldn't dwell on the cross. If it came into my mind, I'd whisper "Thank you Jesus" and then try to quickly think of something else. Still, the memory of the very real, very descriptive lesson of the Crucifixion never dimmed. It remained and remains as precise today as if I just learned about it last Saturday.

And so whenever I would see someone wearing a crucifix as jewelry, I wondered why in the world they wanted to wear such a bitter reminder? Then I would remind myself that this was something that I might be able to better understand once I got a little older.

I didn't see crucifixes worn as jewelry at the Robison's church but they sure talked a lot about Christ's death on the cross. It seemed to me that folks would want to put the matter out of their mind and concentrate on more pleasant things but there were a lot of references to it and phrases like, "He died for me". I knew it, they knew it, we all knew it -- why did they have to keep bringing it up again and again?

They sang all the time about Jesus dying for them, for us. I wondered if I would ever get to a place in my life when the death of Jesus was something I could relax and sing about. It was all I could do to not start crying at the very thought of His death. Singing about it (some of the melodies were slow and the words incredibly sad) brought emotions into my life that were new and somewhat confusing. When the songs about His death were lively, I knew I had a long way to go before I would be as comfortable with the gory details of my redemption as these Christians seemed to be. I was sure that this was something that I'd find an answer to if I kept reading the Bible and listening to more testimonies and 'specials' in song.

In addition to the Robison family, the kind people who attended their church, and the fact that it was there that I secured a Bible, one of the very best things about this Church of the Nazarene was the giant sized cross that hung at the front of the sanctuary. It was an empty cross! Jesus was not there. That was a wonderful relief as compared to my experiences inside the Catholic churches of my childhood from fifth grade onward. I loved that in this church the cross served to remind us that something else, something so much better, happened afterward.

🕊 🕊 🕊

Chapter 14

SAINT TERESA THE PROTESTANT CATHOLIC

What was it about the little church that drew me back as often as I could convince Mother that I wanted to spend the weekend in Webb City with the Robisons? The curiosity factor had been satisfied after the second or third visit.

It took no time at all to conclude that this was not a Catholic church, not a mass, and nothing anywhere close to resembling one. But I decided that it was alright, that there were different ways of going to church and I was just learning about a new one. Surely there was no harm in expanding my horizons if it meant learning how to be a better girl, one that God could be proud of. But first I would need to read more of the stolen Bible, then get myself to a church, to a priest, confess my sin, be forgiven, do some penance, and ask for a Bible for Christmas.

I never heard anyone at the Robison's church refer to themselves or others as Protestant. I decided that that was a term invented and regularly tossed about by Catholics as a way of distinguishing themselves from the rest of the world – from the group who originally protested against ancient ritual; who were rebels liking change more than they liked tradition, and who did not attend the mass. Wait a minute – that was me! Maybe I'd been a Protestant all along and just didn't know it. I wondered if it was possible to be a Protestant Catholic. Did I have to be one or the other? Couldn't I be both?

I knew that if I were older and had a car to drive, I would drive to Webb City's Sacred Heart Catholic Church for catechism, confession, and mass every week and I would get out early enough on Sunday to attend the Robison's worship services. I wanted to be both. I could hyphenate it like some women did their maiden and married names: Teresa the Protestant-Catholic girl, or even Teresa the Catholic/Protestant Saint. I was really getting to know and to love these Christian people but I wasn't ready to compromise my sainty intentions or alter any plans as they related to my eternal future. Heaven (whether Protestant or Catholic) forbid!

Whether it was Catholic or Protestant thinking, I had come to some important conclusions about what I believed and I didn't see how my choice of churches would change the important beliefs that I held. For example, early on I figured out how to be happy instead of sad and how to 'move on' as my dad would say whenever things were about to change in our lives. I figured out that nothing lasts forever – not a school year or a great movie or a favorite pair of shoes; not a delicious meal or a good book or a number one song. Part of growing up is learning that everything comes to an end. Even more important is learning that since there's nothing you can do to change things, there's no use in being a big baby about it. How does a person keep from fussing and crying and feeling horribly sad when something has to end? For me it simply involved reminding myself that when God created everything else, He also created Eternity.

Eternity might sound like one little word but to me it meant World Without End, Amen. No one says goodbye in Eternity. No one has to start over again or relearn things in Eternity. No one wishes they could go back in time or back to another place they once lived. God's Eternity is the only thing in existence without a last day or last time. I knew that someday after this life on earth was finished I'd begin my life in Eternity and all I'd have to do to get there was to be a good girl, then a good teenager, a good adult, and then a good old woman while I was here on earth. I was especially glad to have figured out that if you know that you're on your way to being a saint, you don't have to worry about whether or not you're being good. If I were writing the dictionary, I'd write that the definition of Eternity is: Forever, and that Saint is another word for Good. It didn't matter to me whether this belief was Catholic or Protestant. It was my belief and I wasn't looking to change anything as important as my world without end, amen.

If I absolutely had to choose churches, which would it be? That was a question that I hoped no one would ever ask. It was a question that I refused to give much thought to. I liked both equally and I decided to believe that it is allowable to be just as Protestant as you are Catholic and to love the Catholic Church as much as you love the Protestant church. Despite what I had heard from Julie's sister about excommunication, I wasn't terribly worried about losing my standing within the Catholic faith (especially since I viewed it as somewhat doomed anyway due to my poor attendance, or rather, non-attendance). I didn't worry that in visiting the Robison's Protestant Church of the Nazarene that I might be forfeiting my potential for sainthood. I thought it would be wonderful to continue on the Catholic road to Heaven while occasionally hop scotching over to the Protestant path that Brother Robison and his congregation trekked with such enthusiasm.

I carried 'my' Bible to their church whenever I had opportunity to spend the weekend and by this time I'd 'owned' it for almost two months. Every night I laid in bed and read until I couldn't keep my eyes open any longer and then I would put the Bible under my pillow, turn out the light, and hold tightly to my little plastic crucifix as it glowed in the dark.

I was excited to read Bible stories that I already knew about, having learned them in catechism. I was amazed to learn new things, particularly that it is rightly called The Word of God because it contains lots of red-lettered statements made by Jesus when He was here on earth. Reading the Old Testament, I learned so much about who God is, what He likes and doesn't like, and what He wants for us do. I already knew about having a personal relationship with Jesus and reading The New Testament took away any doubts I might have had about the life that Jesus wants us to live.

In the middle of the Bible I found the most wonderful, most beautiful collection of prayers. They read like poems and like songs and there are 150 of them! Actually, 148 because the first two Psalms seemed to be important lessons that we need to learn before we can start in on the next part. The rest of Psalms are prayers in words that I'd felt in my heart but had never been able to express so honestly or so desperately to God. They didn't seem like something I could memorize but I wanted to read and re-read them every day for the rest of my life. I enjoyed reading them aloud as if I was praying to God.

When I read the New Testament for the first time, I thought about my long-time-ago-friend Julie and wished that I could tell her that the prayer we call the Our Father is a prayer that everybody seems to know, even people who aren't Catholics. They call it The Lord's Prayer and it's the same words that we've always said. She and her older sister Jana would probably be shocked if I was able to show them that this prayer is actually in the Bible, in red letters, because the first person who ever prayed it was Jesus.

This Bible education was something I had never expected and something that never stopped filling me with anticipation and excitement. I didn't know that it was possible to hunger for anything except food and now I had a hunger for anything and everything I could read between the covers of this tattered and previously well used Bible. Everything I read seemed like nourishment and then anything from the book of Psalms was like desert. Usually, just before I'd fall asleep, I would tell myself that I needed to be sure and confess my sin of thievery. As much as I loved reading The Word of God, I expected that I would enjoy it even more once I was forgiven for stealing it out from under the guy whose name was on the inside cover. Yes, I needed to try to become heartly sorry and to get myself into a confessional.

And then the Catholic priest showed up at our house for a visit.

🕊 🕊 🕊

Chapter 15

FATHER CONFESSOR

Father Palermo did not own an automobile. He pedaled an old bicycle the ten miles or so into Oronogo, stopped at the little Post Office to ask where the Prins family lives, and showed up unannounced late one afternoon while I was helping mother fix supper.

Despite the fact that he was more than twice my age, watching him from where I stood at the kitchen window, he looked like someone I might have a class with at school. Sacred Heart Catholic Church must have been his first assignment. He was rail thin with dark wavy hair and on closer inspection he looked like a college kid except that he was dressed in black slacks and a black button down shirt with the white collar that priests wear.

When I answered the front door, he removed a faded black baseball cap from his head. I was taller than he and probably outweighed him by a dozen pounds. I imagined that he stayed slender by riding that bicycle or maybe he was on the road to sainthood and, just as I used to drink glass after glass of water, praying that it would become wine, perhaps he fasted. I supposed that the recipe for sainthood differs according to the individual. It crossed my mind that I hadn't prayed my water-into-wine prayer for more months than I could recall.

The young priest introduced himself and apologized for not having visited sooner. He said that he was going to be leaving the Webb City church to move to Arizona but that he wanted to come by to tell us about a family who lived somewhere near us who sometimes attended Sacred Heart. He said that maybe they would be willing to drive us to mass whenever they attended. He couldn't remember their name but thought it was McGraves or maybe it was McGrove. I asked if they had any children but Father Palermo wasn't sure. I got the feeling that they rarely attended church and that he had not yet spoken with them about this carpooling idea.

Mother responded by stating that we had not become acquainted with any families in Oronogo. If there were any other Catholics, we didn't know them. We hadn't actually met anyone at all in our town with the exception of the lady who worked at the post office. I usually made small talk with area kids while waiting for the school bus, but going to church was never a topic of conversation. It was no exaggeration to describe the little town of Oronogo as deathly quiet; people seemed to keep to themselves. They probably avoided 'the family that moved in from California' and who could blame them? After all, we Prinses came with a cloud of mystery surrounding us; I mean, why would anyone move from sun shiny San Diego to this ghost town whose existence wasn't even map worthy? Mother and I felt this way but we didn't burden the priest with our woes.

Father Palermo was sort of like The Welcome Wagon. It was great to finally have someone knock on our door and want to get to know us (even if he was getting ready to move out of state). He had a friendly smile and dark, expressive eyes. He seemed kind and supportive of Mother as she explained to him that she had plans to "get us to church" but that we were "still adjusting to the move from the suburbs out west to being out here in the country". She told him about dad who was "gone with his job so much of the time", who was not a Catholic, and who drove the only car that we owned. I sort of laughed when she told him that she didn't know how to drive and didn't have a driver's license (as if she thought that this bike riding priest was going to give her a car).

Father Palermo seemed to give off an air of kindness and mercy mixed with a generous dose of sympathy. He nodded and said "I see" and "Oh, yes" until mother finally finished her apologetics. She proudly reported that we'd all been baptized, that five of her six children had received their first Holy Communion, and that her two oldest had been Confirmed. Suddenly Mother's eyes widened and her face seemed to indicate that she had come up with a brilliant idea. She had conceived of a way to take the spotlight off of herself and point it directly on to me. With a smile cast in my direction and look of relief, she announced, "My Tess here should be studying for her Confirmation but I don't know for sure what she is going to do."

I was ready. I could start by asking why in the world there was no Catholic Church in Oronogo and describe how I was stranded out here and unable to continue with my catechism studies. I'd ask how he found out about us and maybe I would ask why the McGraves or McGroves hadn't been by to meet us. I'd tell him that if it was *our* family, we would have already brought a cake or a pie to the new people in town and we'd have already invited them to walk, or ride or whatever to church with us. Well, maybe we wouldn't have done any of that but it would definitely have crossed our mind and our intentions would have been good ones. Before I could organize my thoughts into a presentable challenge, Father Palermo rose from the easy chair recliner where he'd been sitting and walked across the room to sit down beside me on the sofa.

He bent forward and leaned toward me, sort of angling his head to one side as if he expected me to speak in a whisper. It was as if he was assuming that whatever I was preparing to say was going to have such a tremendous impact that he wanted to be close enough to catch every word. Ah ha! I decided that I must be giving off some kind of sainty vibe that only a Holy Ordered person would recognize. He must have sensed that although I was not yet a saint, I was on my way to the honor. Yes, this young rookie priest must have been aware that he was sitting in the presence of a multiple miracle recipient!

In accordance with my upbringing, I decided to let him speak first. He could start by letting me know that he knew I'd been blessed or he could begin by asking me to tell about my miracles. He could have been very casual and cool and said something like, "So what's going on in your world?" or "What are your plans Teresa?" Instead, he looked me right in the eyes, lowered his voice to a true whisper and gently demanded, "Daughter, when was your last confession?"

Suddenly the chilly late-autumn air seemed to switch to a heat wave resembling those wildly hot Santa Anna winds that blow the most unexpected things into one's path. At that moment Father Palermo didn't look like a youthful, energetic bike riding college guy in a priest outfit. He looked like the dozens of ageless clergy men and women I'd come into contact with throughout my Catholic upbringing. Now he was like all the others – not especially old, not especially young, neither masculine nor feminine. He didn't look like someone who might experience occasional outbursts of laughter or unexpected tears, unexplainable cravings, or personal likes and dislikes. In that moment he was the Church's ambassador to a woman and her daughter who'd relocated to Missouri less than four months prior to his visit.

"Daughter, when was your last confession?" He had asked the question as if his whole purpose for existing depended on my answer. His expression was strained and serious, almost as if he suddenly realized how worn out he was from the long bike ride. It is no exaggeration to say that in my mind he looked as if he would have somehow been physically wounded had I failed to give an honest reply.

I was too flustered to come up with the "Bless me Father for I have sinned, my last confession was about a hundred and twenty something weeks ago." I certainly didn't have the spur-of-the-moment mathematical acuity to announce that it was approaching one thousand days since I'd made my last confession. I needed to think fast but nothing clever came to mind.

And so, I lowered my head and just let the words fall out of my mouth. I told the truth, the whole truth, and nothing but the truth about how I had stolen a Bible. As bad as this sin was, I knew it didn't matter how long it had been since my last confession; that wasn't the issue at hand. He had come to give me the opportunity to spill my guts, to evaluate the contents, and to see what would unfold as a result. I didn't care if the penance was going to be a hundred and twenty something Act of Contrition prayers. I just wanted to finally get the sin out from inside of me and into the air that surrounded the only person who could give me the kind of absolution I needed for sainthood. I'd already discussed the matter with God and had asked Him to forgive me for being so selfish, but I still held a strong belief that forgiveness by the Catholic Church would be necessary as well, particularly for a sin as heinous as thievery.

Would I lose out on my lifelong dream? Would I not only be excommunicated but also be informed that, under these mortal-sin-circumstances, it was unforgivable? Was I to learn that I was doomed no matter what? Was he going to further condemn me for having an appetite for kissing boys? I made a quick decision to totally avoid the subject of kissing and chose instead to focus my confession solely on my grievously sinful nature as a robber of church property.

I told Father Palermo everything as it happened. I told him that I read the Bible every single night. I told him how that sometimes on the weekends I would stay in my room and read chapter after chapter because I knew that I was eventually going to have to give the Bible back. I told him that even though what I read was a lot of history, it always seemed as if I could relate it to things that were happening in my own life. I just couldn't say enough about the thrill of having so important a book in my possession. I knew I was talking too fast and that it really didn't sound like I was sorry for what I'd done but I didn't care how fanatical I sounded. Father Palermo had said that he was moving away, so it wasn't like I was going to have another opportunity to get this said and done.

I told him that although I knew I should be ashamed, I usually didn't feel that way. I confessed that my unrepentant attitude was probably a bigger sin than the stealing. I admitted that I didn't want to make it right by returning the Bible. I told him that I could probably find a way to get a new Bible of my own, maybe for Christmas, but I'd grown attached to the one I stole. I had even taken the liberty of underlining some verses in pencil.

Father Palermo listened intently as I rambled on and on. His face showed that he was devoting every ounce of his energy to attending to my confession. Still, he never spoke a word in reply to my sinfulness. Instead, he questioned me about the church I'd been attending. He asked if they served communion, if they observed the sacrament of Baptism. He asked a couple of questions about the preacher. Always appearing as if he would wait patiently for my responses, I continued to blurt out my answers without a second thought.

When he asked what I was currently reading in the Bible, I gave him an exuberant report about the first and second books of Samuel in the Old Testament; about the stories of David the shepherd boy and his devotion to his best friend Jonathan. The way I told him about David's marriage to a woman named Michael and then his sinfulness with Bathsheba made it sound as if it was the gossip of the day right here in 1968. I talked about David becoming the king of Israel after such a struggle. I thrilled in telling how, despite his sinfulness, God continued to love David. With incredible grace this priest listened as if he was hearing the stories for the first time.

I used my face, my hands, and my voice to retell stories about the miracles that I had read. This was the first opportunity I'd had to recite my lessons and I was savoring the moment. I suspected that I was entertaining the priest with my unbridled vivacity, leaving all hint of shyness behind me. I was on a roll and it felt right. Meanwhile, Mother sat across the room with her eyebrows drawn together in a confused look. She stared at me as if I had just landed smack dab in the middle of her living room in a space ship from some far away universe and was speaking a language that she didn't understand. I think she was wishing that she could be anywhere but in the midst of this very unusual confession scene.

Outside the window it looked as if it was nearing dusk. A thought crossed my mind of him riding that old bicycle home after sundown. Dressed in such dark colors, it would be difficult for drivers to see him. Not only that, but the roads between Oronogo and Webb City were covered with pot-holes where over time the ground had given way under the weight of the blacktop. Where there were no holes in the road, there were sharp curves and a little one-lane bridge without side rails to guide you toward the middle. And so, in a somewhat cocky tone of voice I concluded my presentation. I expected that the final act of this incredible experience would be Father Palermo becoming the stern, judgmental, formal, solemn type of priest of which I was more accustomed.

We both knew that I was not a pure bred Catholic. I was not a faithful attendee of the mass. I was A.W.O.L. when it came to reporting for duty as a soldier in Christ's army via the sacrament of Confirmation. Still, I had the nerve to disrespect his Holy Orders by winding up our time together saying, "Father Palermo, in the New Testament book of Matthew there is a report about when Jesus was talking to the people. He told them that it was wrong to call anyone Father. He said that only God should be called Father. What do you think about that?" Before he had even a fraction of a second to respond, I added, "What do you think about how the Bible talks about going directly to God with our petitions? It says that the only intermediary between God and man is Jesus. What do you think about that?" At rapid-fire pace I added, "And another thing, there are places in the Bible that say that no one is without sin. It says that Jesus is the only one who ever lived in the world without sinning."

I was fully prepared to go get the Bible from under my pillow and show him exactly where these words were but somehow I knew it wouldn't be necessary. Now I waited for his response. With a kindly but very serious look on his face, Father Palermo stood to his feet, reached downward and took my hand in his. He held it as if we were going to shake hands but he didn't let go. He placed his other hand on top of our handshake. And then he smiled. His face was so kind and his expression was comfortable as if I had just told him that around the corner there's a huge, fluffy white cloud waiting for him to flop down on and rest for a while.

He smiled with a genuine happiness in his expression and he looked as if he understood every word that I had so haphazardly spoken. With a nod of his head he looked me square in the eyes and said "Teresa, keep on reading The Bible. Keep on praying to God and pray to Jesus as well. It is good that you are devoting yourself to the study of our Lord."

He let go of my hand and walked toward the door. Then he turned around, remembering that he'd left his ball cap on the easy chair. Looking at Mother, he smiled and said "God bless you and your family". Mother followed him to the front yard gate where his bike rested against the wrought iron fence.

As I watched him walk away, I thought about a million things I should have said. I wished that I'd told him about the songs they sing at the Robison's church – songs about how they know for sure, without a doubt, with blessed assurance that their sins are forgiven and that they are someday going to be in Heaven. I wished that I'd thought to tell him that the people at the Robison's church never seemed like they were wondering if they were good enough for God to love them.

When Father Palermo was out of sight, I turned from the window and asked, "What did you do Mother? Call Sacred Heart and ask them to send the priest to tell me to quit going to the Robison's church?" Mother promised that she had nothing to do with his visit. I believed her. I decided that it was God who sent this man to our house on that November afternoon.

As a representative of the Catholic Church, he had certain responsibilities but who would have found out if he'd decided on that day to be cold or intolerant, maybe a little rude or uncaring? Instead, he was the very image of kindness and patience. Considering the fact that he was on his way out of Missouri, he could have made the visit brief but he stayed for nearly three hours. He would have gotten away with it had he represented the church in a way that no one would have ever discovered, and maybe that is exactly what he did: He didn't patronize my youthfulness. He didn't judge or scold me. Without speaking more than a handful of words he led me to spill out the contents of my heart and to work out for myself the course that I would need to take to make things right. He didn't excommunicate me and never commented on my sinfulness. He didn't name off a list of prayer-book-prayers for me to say as penance.

This young priest knew that I was not yet heartly sorry and so he didn't intercede to God on my behalf for forgiveness. But then again, I never asked him to. I didn't actually make a Catholic confession and he didn't voice a Catholic absolution. I guess he knew that when the time was right I would go directly to the Author of forgiveness. I would not require the assistance of a priest, a nun, or even a saint. The fact of the matter was that my last Catholic confession had been nearly one hundred and thirty weeks ago. It was during Father Palermo's visit that I realized I'd never again find it necessary to enter a tiny confessional to ask a priest to seek forgiveness on my behalf.

I never saw Father Palermo again. By the time I finally set foot in Sacred Heart Catholic Church, he had already left for his new appointment.

🕊 🕊 🕊

Chapter 16

EXTRAORDINARY PEOPLE

Snow covered the ground and huge icicles hung like Christmas ornaments around the eaves of our house. I was living in a crystal and white wintertime that I'd only seen in books and in the summer following 6th grade when my Aunt Myrna took me to see the movie Dr. Zhivago.

On some days school was called off because the old busses couldn't risk trying to make it across our little bridges and around the wicked curves along the country roads. This was November and true winter was still to come.

Just before the worst of the weather set, in I got to spend a Saturday and Sunday at Merlyna's house and make another visit to her church. Figuring it might be my last chance until who-knows-when, I decided to confess my wayward behavior to Brother Robison. That way, if he told me to never darken the door of their home and church again, I'd start working on a different plan for my life and set it into motion with the coming of the new year. I wanted to confess, apologize, and try to get the Robison's forgiveness before Christmas came around so that I could enjoy the holiday without all the guilt that had become such a normal part of my life.

I sat across the dining table and told Merlyna's dad what I had done. He listened with a very serious look on his face and then told me that I should talk to Ann about it but that he was sure she'd given me a Bible from the shelf that held the old books that were no longer used. He explained that sometimes when church members got a new Bible, they would bring their old one to the church because they didn't want to throw it away and there was always the chance that someone might come to church and forget to bring theirs or that a visitor might not own one. He looked at the Bible and said that I was welcome to keep it. He said that the man whose name was written inside of the front cover was not around anymore but that he had "probably owned two or three new Bibles since this one". As he stood to leave the table, Brother Robison smiled at me, patted my arm, and said, "You're a good girl. You know we all love you."

At Sunday School the next morning I told Ann that I'd talked to Brother Robison about the Bible she had 'given me' a few months back. She told me that the books on that particular shelf had been there for years "but no one wants to throw them away, especially not the Bibles".

Ann thought the whole thing was funny but I don't think I will ever forget Brother Robison's reaction on that Saturday when I sat across the table from him and assumed that he was the one who could help to make right the wrong inside of me. As always, he was kind in a fatherly sort of way but the expression on his face had seemed to say, "It doesn't matter if what you took was a penny or a crumb of bread; if it didn't belong to you and you believed that it belonged to someone else but took it anyway – that is a sin and it is not the way that we live in this house, in this church, in this world". His gentleness and concern for my life meant so much. His way of life caused me to consider that since Jesus is no longer here on earth in the flesh, maybe there are people who love Him enough to want to be just like Him, to be His representatives and to show people what He would do or say in any given situation. It wasn't necessary for Brother Robison to scold or to advise me; I got it. I understood that even if no one was injured, damage was done and it mustn't ever happen again.

December arrived and I turned fifteen years old. If I wasn't ready for sainthood now, I probably never would be. Although it occupied my mind a bit less than in previous years, I wasn't ready to give up hope on becoming a saint. I was doubtful, however, that there was a single Catholic in the world who would put in a good word for me or persuade the powers that be to vote me into the ranks. I imagined that even my friend Julie would have changed her mind if she knew what I'd become – a girl whose confession included breaking commandments as a liar and a thief, a girl who likes kisses more than convents, and who'd rather be decked out in a mini-skirt than in nun-wear.

Being snowed-in and unable to attend school gave me time to think about what I'd read concerning the requirements of sainthood. Indeed you do have to die before the church will canonize you and getting the church to make that happen can take years and years. By the time they got finished with me, I wouldn't have been just dead and gone, I'd be long gone and forgotten.

Apparently, in order to be named a saint someone has to recommend you and a lengthy investigation is conducted to inquire about the miracles or incredible events that may have taken place during your lifetime. Next, and this is a part that really troubled me, a group of church leaders and invited guests get together and do what they call 'Playing Devil's Advocate'. They discuss and then debate the validity of the experiences that may or may not qualify a person for sainthood. Why did they have to call it by that name? Why couldn't they call it something like The Verdict is Yours? Why did they have to bring the devil into the discussion? I bet he loved that they called it 'playing'. I had strong feelings about the matter but voicing them might have automatically disqualified me for the honor of sainthood.

I could think of a bunch of people, siblings included, who would have had a heyday offering opinions about my two miracles. Next, after the debate team finishes up, more meetings are held and attempts are made to authenticate the miracles until finally the pope either gives his consent or he disapproves the recommendation. If the pope decides that the nominee should be named as a saint, a date is set on the calendar for the saint's feast day and every year on that date the saint is remembered for her (or his, of course) miraculous life. People throughout the world pray to the saint on my (I mean his or her) particular feast day and some churches (probably the ones I attended as a child) hold special celebrations. Oh, wow! How great that would be! I wondered if anyone was already using December 22nd (my birthday) as a feast day. I also liked September 23rd as it is the first day of autumn, but I wouldn't be choosy; every day is a holiday if you're a saint!

On the other hand, what a letdown to go through the lengthy process only to end up with a 'no' vote. I guess maybe it's a good thing that you're dead if the vote doesn't go your way. I wondered how many other religious denominations had saints and if their route to greatness was swifter and less complicated.

I thought about the people that Merlyna's father referred to as saints. What was it about their lives that earned them such a lofty title? With all due respect, they were just regular folk unless maybe they had received miracles but were keeping them 'hush-hush' just as I was doing at this point in my life. I enjoyed Merlyna's company but I never told her or any new friend about my miracles.

At the Robison's church the testimonies told of poor health, rebellious children, or personal struggles overcoming the consequences of previous sinful choices. Still, they were happy people despite their difficulties. They seemed to have normal, everyday lives with everyday problems but somehow they still smiled and laughed had a huge amount of joy. It was as if the bigger their struggle, the more their love for God outweighed the problem. That is what was so unique about them. They weren't like the martyrs who basically said to trouble "Bring it on". No, these people clearly hated their problems but they loved their God who gave them strength to make it through each day without letting the problems get the best of them. Somehow, they'd found a way to overcome the rotten parts of life by focusing instead on the sweetness of God. I understood what they believed while at the same time wondering how they were able to actually 'live it out' in real life.

I came to the conclusion that if God wanted me for one of His saints, He'd bring about miracle number three right away before the end of the year, and I wouldn't worry whether or not the church would come through for me after I died. In the meantime I would take every opportunity to continue to watch these living saints to see if there was any possibility that I might eventually come around to catching some of their joy. It sure seemed contagious but nothing that good could come to a person very easily. Surely there was a hidden cost that I would learn about eventually.

One thing was sure, I wasn't going to fret over my history as a Bible thief. After telling Brother Robison what I'd done, I talked to God about it, said The Act of Contrition, and then I assigned my own penance – the hardest penance I'd ever done. It was to put the Bible back onto the shelf after the worship service that Sunday morning. Now my conscience would have to find something else to bother me about and when the weather cleared I'd have to see if public libraries have Bibles for check-out.

🕊 🕊 🕊

Chapter 17

IN THE GARDEN

By comparison to the teenagers Mother watched on the soap operas or on the movie screen, I was what you'd call a 'good girl' who never got into trouble. I made good grades in school and fit in with the crowd.

I was fairly popular but I always figured that it was because I had three very attractive brothers whom the girls wanted to date and the guys wanted to befriend. I hadn't ever been in the kind of trouble that puts parents to shame or that could make a family want to pack up and move to another town. I'd put my thieving days behind me before my family even caught wind of my fall from grace. Still, when I was required to sit and think about my life, I felt as worthless as the road kill I'd stare at when riding the bus to school each morning.

The latest trend in education was called Humanities. It appeared that the purpose was to teach us to inspect our own life and to judge ourselves so that we'd be sensitive and fair at observing and judging others. In writing class we had to create our obituary and epitaphs and then read them to the group. I was uncomfortable with this kind of schooling. I liked to be self-centered, but I didn't want anyone to know about it and I certainly didn't want my teachers to make it a homework assignment. They called it 'self-evaluation' and 'seeking one's identity' with the goal of demonstrating what unique and yet very similar people we are.

Maybe I took the whole thing too seriously, but what the humanities did for me was to make me feel doomed to a difficult life. Worse than that, the studies caused me to feel horribly ashamed for things I'd never done – things that had happened in decades and centuries past. I'd been brought up in a setting where the phrases "your conscience will bother you" and "guilty conscience" were tossed around regularly. Now I was sitting in public school classes learning how to apply my guilty conscience to just about every bad thing that had happened since life began. I loved to study history, but I sure hated feeling responsible for what took place. On one day we might learn that we are uniquely individual with exclusive ideas and the next day we would read that we are just a tiny speck of dust in this gigantic cosmos. Maybe I wasn't mature enough for this type of learning. I made great grades and thought of myself as above average in intellect, creativity, and a dozen other areas but now I'd found another subject that was too weighty for my ninth grade brain. Now I was becoming a math and a humanities reject.

During Holy week, the days that lead up to Easter Sunday, I devised a secret plan to finally visit Sacred Heart Catholic Church. It was located less than a half mile from the high school and only blocks from the public library. I got permission to walk to the library after school one day. My sister and her boyfriend had agreed to drive me home around 5:30 after they finished their extracurricular activities. That would give me just under two hours for my long awaited adventure.

All week long I was excited as I waited for Friday to arrive. I felt as if I was someone who had been away for a long time and was finally coming home for a visit to a house I'd never actually seen. I could hardly wait to sit in a pew at the front of the sanctuary and look at everything around me. Then I'd walk around and touch the feet of each of the saint statues. It was something that I had always done and although I never knew for sure why I was doing it, it always had a very special meaning to me. I planned to move slowly to look at each of the stained glass windows and to finally stand and pray in front of each of the Stations of the Cross. The stations are depictions of the events that took place leading up to Jesus's burial. The first one is when He was condemned to die and the last one shows Him being placed in the tomb. As far back as when I was in the third or fourth grade, I'd wished that there were a few more stations so that I could see when the tomb was empty and when his friends and family saw that He was alive, and maybe one that showed Him ascending into Heaven.

Sacred Heart Church was bound to have statues and stained glass that would differ from the churches in California. Perhaps it would have a smaller or more contemporary altar area and new mysteries for me to view and to try and solve. Still, I expected there to be similarities. I could hardly wait to breathe in the atmosphere of the church and the incense; the atmosphere of reverence and solitude. I wanted to remind my senses of the glorious feeling of being in the midst of the saints whose statues were there to protect the church and to inspire the parishioners. Friday was going to be a very important day. I was looking forward to finally feeling that strong, invisible embrace of the familiar.

It was Good Friday, just two days before Easter. I opened the heavy wooden doors of the church and walked in with confidence, as if I was a member, as if I knew my way around. The entire sanctuary was lit by only three candles in tall red votives at the front altar area. Except for the bits of sunlight poking through the stained glass windows, the church was almost as dark as a cave. I was immediately stunned to discover that I was not going to see the beauty of the sanctuary as it was almost entirely covered in black cloth. Even the large crucifix hanging on the far wall of the altar was draped in black. I had completely forgotten the tradition of covering everything from Good Friday until Easter Sunday. On Sunday, during the sunrise mass, the sanctuary would return it its usual beauty in celebration of Christ's resurrection from the dead. That was always a glorious time but right now it was Friday and the church resembled The Tomb because it was supposed to.

Three hundred and sixty three days a year the church looked like a palace or maybe what Heaven might be like. Of all the days to visit Sacred Heart, I came on one of the two when everything is draped in black. I had been learning in school about the randomness of everything, how that nothing happens by Providence or destiny. Everything was hit-or-miss, it just happened and that's how the universe works. As I sat in the darkness of the church, I would have bet my life that there was a Divine reason that on this day of all days, when I had finally found a way to get inside of Sacred Heart Catholic Church, there were no saint statues to welcome me, no adorned altar area. Yes, there was a reason for this and it didn't matter that I was unsure just what that reason might be.

On a table near the door was a small stack of papers that looked like the order of the mass for the previous Sunday. There was also a stack of what looked like church announcements or newsletters and a little wooden tray with a couple dozen prayer cards and bookmarks. I reached in and chose one that had a picture of Christ praying in the Garden of Gethsemane. I sat down at the back of the church, set the bookmark in my lap, and stared at it. I knew the story that went along with the picture. I'd learned about it in catechism when we studied what was called The Passion of Christ.

I thought about how the picture would make a beautiful stained glass window but wait, didn't one of the churches I used to attend have a stained glass window portraying Jesus in the garden? I couldn't remember for sure but how could I have forgotten? A wave of sadness started at the top of my head and swept downward, settling in my lap where the bookmark lay.

I did what I'd always done when I would begin to feel downhearted – I used my imagination to take me somewhere other than where I was at that moment. I put myself inside of the picture, inside of the Garden of Gethsemane. I imagined that I walked into the garden. The grass was sort of wet because it was dusk. I know the trees, they are olive trees. I am moving very quietly, approaching Jesus. I'm not wearing my avocado and brown plaid jumper, knee socks, and tennies. I'm wearing a whitish-tan colored gown and leather sandals. I'm dressed like Jesus, except in girl clothes. I have the idea that I will kneel beside Him and lean to the left so that I can rest my head against His arm. Maybe I am going to put one of my hands near His as He has them folded in prayer atop a big stone.

As I picture myself tip-toeing toward Him, I realize how unworthy I am to even be in the garden where He is. Maybe I would get into trouble for trespassing. Now I imagine myself an intruder, afraid to move toward Him but even more fearful of turning back. My mind sort of wanders a bit and I realize that I finally understand the words that are said at mass just prior to receiving communion, "Lord, I am not worthy…"

Before I can even finish the thought of my unworthiness, I imagine that Jesus speaks to me. He doesn't turn His head to look my way. He stays exactly as He is depicted in the picture on the bookmark. I hear Him say "If you thought yourself worthy, you would not have chosen to come into the garden. It is because you are unworthy that you came along beside Me. That is why I am here. That is why I am praying."

Wow! What had just happened? Did I imagine that? Did I actually hear that? Was that my voice thinking out loud or is that what Jesus sounds like when He speaks? Was that the best job my imagination had ever done or what?! I got up quickly to leave the church and as I stepped into the light of late afternoon, I realized that I might have to run to get to the library before Sharron and Danny got there.

As I waited for my ride, I thought about what Jesus had said. I told myself that I would need to spend a lot of time deciding what it all meant. Sitting on the front steps of the library, I realized that I wasn't a little catechism-kid anymore. I needed to grow up and start thinking like a fifteen year old. There was no need to avoid self-evaluation and a search for identity if I used the lessons to bring me closer to being the person God wanted me to be. I wondered what would happen next. I wondered if it was possible to get to a place in my life where I could imagine walking into the garden without feeling unworthy. Was that allowable? Are we allowed to imagine ourselves smack dab in the presence of Jesus without a guilty conscience?

🕊 🕊 🕊

Chapter 18

WAIST DEEP IN WASTE

It amazed me that when I was inside of Sacred Heart Catholic Church, the thought of being a saint never once entered my mind. What that meant was that for the first time I could recall, I was in a Catholic Church and didn't long for the day that I could be one of the beautiful, pastel-painted, haloed statues.

For as long as I could remember I had wanted to be famous; to be noticed, to be thought of as one of God's favorites. I was the shy child lost in the middle of an outspoken, high energy family of eight. I didn't want to be thought of as 'Richard's little sister', or as 'one of the Prins kids', or 'that girl from California'. For so long I had wanted to be Saint somebody or other. Then we moved to Missouri. Then I got a little older. Then I read the Bible and saw a different way of loving God, a different way of belonging to a church. I no longer wanted the spotlight to someday shine on me. I didn't want to have a sainty glow that people would most likely have been afraid to approach. If it was possible for God to give off light, I wanted to live my life in *that* light. I wasn't totally clear on this concept, but I'd gotten some ideas about it from Brother Robison's preaching.

I had adored the mysteries and the dimly lit sanctuary that was the Catholic Church of my childhood. I enjoyed not knowing why rituals were performed. It thrilled me to hear statements made in Latin rather than in English; it didn't matter that I didn't have a clue what the words meant. But things changed and now I found myself laughing at how consumed I had been in pursuing sainthood. These days, I rarely thought about the halo, the statues, or my picture on a prayer card. Now I wanted to understand the meaning of new words like Christianity, conversion, redemption, salvation, holiness. These words didn't sound musical or poetic to my ears. Now I was hearing words that sounded powerful and very important.

When I got home from my trip to the church and the library, I asked Mother if I could spend the night at Merlyna's on Saturday. I didn't say anything about 'Merlyna's church' or refer to it as the Robison's. I still wasn't attending very often, but I'd come to think of it as *my* church as well as theirs. I told mother that starting right now, if anyone asked me I where I went to church, I was going to say that I go to Webb City Nazarene on Tenth Street. This was a major declaration because all we had ever been was Catholic. The reason we hadn't set foot in any other church was because it never occurred to us that we had a choice. Just as we had not chosen our country or our family, I had always thought that our religion was something we were born with like brown eyes or a space between your two front teeth.

Deciding to make the Robison's church my church was bold and very much unlike the 'go with the flow' daughter that Mother was accustomed to.

This way of thinking came as a surprise to me because I'd always been so cautious, fearing that it would result in our family moving away if I dared to claim anything as mine, if I ever got "too attached" as Mother would say. "So tell me now, Mom, are we going to move away in a couple years?" That seemed like the appropriate question for this particular discussion. Why? Because if Mother was opposed to my being a part of a Protestant church, she would find comfort in knowing that we'd be relocating away from that church in about two years. I couldn't tell for certain, but it looked as if Mother was sad when she answered, "No. No more moving. Not this time Tess. We won't be moving away from here. This is where your dad plans to stay."

I didn't know if I should celebrate that we'd never have to pack up and move out or if I should detest the thought of never again living near the ocean. I decided to shelve the news about never leaving Oronogo in favor of thinking about what had taken place at Sacred Heart Catholic Church earlier that afternoon. I had a lot to think about and what with my household chores and homework assignments, I wasn't going to get to sort it all out until bedtime or maybe the next day.

I had a dream that night and it was my first-ever dream about Jesus. It was a nightmare. I dreamed that I was standing in a room with dark walls and no lighting. The room was full of poop, or as Mother would call it, B.M. (the disgusting abbreviation for bowel movement). I was in the center of the room and the poop came up to my knees. I won't describe how it looked or smelled; suffice it to say that the dream was very realistic.

I could feel the hardwood floor beneath my feet but I was certain that at some point the floor was going to give way and I would begin sinking as if in quicksand. There at the front of the room, standing behind a tall podium was Jesus. He was dressed exactly as in the bookmark picture of Him in the Garden of Gethsemane. He was standing in a clearing, so to speak. Otherwise, I was alone in the classroom and I knew that Jesus was the teacher.

I spoke out loudly and asked, "Jesus tell me what this means". Jesus said, "You already know what this means". Instantly, even before He had finished speaking, I knew what it meant. I was in Hell. I was standing in Hell.

I said to Jesus, "Hell is human waste. Each person is surrounded by all of the opportunities that they passed up, by all the time they wasted being cruel or unnecessarily angry. The waste is every hateful, hurtful word they ever spoke. Everywhere they look they see another example of something they should have done but they let the moment pass without doing it. All the waste is all the times when they had the chance to make something right but they refused to do it."

I talked about being phony and wasting other people's time by saying things that aren't true. In my dream I was aware that I was learning the lesson in the very instant that the words flowed out of my mouth.

I said that Hell wasn't someone or something torturing you. No, you tortured yourself. You couldn't escape the memories of what you'd done or even of what you had tried to forget that you'd done. The more you stood there surrounded by them, the more they stunk. The longer you stood in Hell, the more wastefulness appeared and the deeper you sunk down into the piles. Now I found myself surrounded up to my waist. It was really bad.

In this Hell you became human waste itself. You live on and on and on, surrounded by the details of your wasted life. Loud sounds of moaning came from the people in other rooms.

Good grief! How could I be fifteen years old and have such a vivid dream about Hell? Was it my Catholic conditioning? Was it just a new aspect of my personality? Was it the result of those humanities studies? Did God know I dreamed this dream? Did He allow it to happen because He saw that I was ready for something so shocking? I guess the dream didn't have an ending because I don't remember any 'happily ever after' or a rescue scene.

I had a feeling that there were others who'd had this very same dream. I'd never heard or read about any of them because, like me, they were unlikely to be telling people about something so gross and at the same time so very fascinating in a scary sort of way. I decided that the dream was like a puzzle that I would put together whenever I got clues about how do to so. I wondered if there was anyone I could speak to about the matter. It was really too disgusting to talk about.

Less than twelve hours later I was sitting at the Robison's dining table telling Brother Robison about my strange and stinking dream. He provided the only listening ears I would dare to tell. He flinched a time or two and seemed somewhat amazed with the details. He didn't get his Bible and show me what it says about the reality of Hell. He didn't tell me that it was similar to or different than his beliefs. He didn't use the occasion as an opportunity to preach to me, nor to say that I was right or wrong. Brother Robison treated the whole thing as if it was no more than a young girl's dream. It looked to me as if he was pleased to have been the one I chose to tell. And it looked as if he was definitely going to continue to pray for his daughter's unusual friend.

By this time I had been visiting the church once or twice a month for about six months. In all of that time he never asked me to change my way of thinking. He never quizzed me on my Catholic upbringing, nor did he or any of his family ever cause me to feel that I was being judged by them. What he did say on that occasion and many others was, "You've gotta trust in God". He never made me feel stupid for being filled with questions that often must have sounded ridiculous. I originally thought that he would make a great Catholic priest but then I wouldn't have had his daughter as my locker partner and friend. If Bob Robison was anything like God the Father, I sure was privileged to know him. And if God the Father was anything like Brother Bob Robison, that would explain why I loved Him so dearly and was so grateful to be His child.

Weeks and even months later I continued to try to understand my dream until I finally decided that it was in my own best interest to stop. The truth of the matter was that I didn't want the dream to apply to my own life and it sickened me to think about it applying to the life of anyone else. On a few occasions I actually thanked God for giving me the dream and then I would apologize in the event that the dream didn't come from Him and that, like me, He didn't care much for its content, nor the retelling of its details. Little did I know that in the years to come I would never again have a dream as vivid or as troubling as the one I'd come to think of as 'waist deep in waste'.

🕊 🕊 🕊

Chapter 19

FINDING MY WAY HOME

Springtime finally arrived in our part of the world after winter seemed to drag on clear into the month of April. When tiny buds began to sprout on the trees and bright yellow flowers pushed their faces up through the melting snow, I got a surge of energy.

I felt as if my spirit or my soul or something deep inside had awakened from a long hibernation. After having lived out west where it felt like summertime all year long, winter had been a cold but beautiful 'first' and now another new season was unfolding.

At our house daffodils seemed to pop up out of nowhere and there were little white star-shaped flowers that covered the front and side yards like a carpet. Later, along the backyard fence, dozens and dozens of lavender, dark purple, and peach colored irises stayed in bloom for months. Springtime brought evidence of what this property had been at one time. Someone had planted lilac bushes and honeysuckle and strongly scented flowering shrubs. It took only a tiny breeze to send the scent of perfume from the yard into the house. I liked the way I was feeling – sort of giddy and borderline mischievous. I wondered if maybe this was what anticipation feels like when you're about to finish your first year of high school.

Winter had provided me with hours of study time. I'd received a Living Bible for Christmas and it was so different than my first Bible that I sometimes wondered if it was allowable (by whom, I don't know) to have this particular version. It was my sister's boyfriend Danny who explained that what I was reading was not an actual literal translation but a modern language paraphrase of the Bible. I sort of understood what he meant, but not really and it seemed uncool to ask him to explain it in words that made more sense to me. I continued to read every night and to learn more about God, what He expects from His people, how He loves us, and how we ought to live. I eventually mustered up the courage to ask Ann if I could borrow-back the Bible from the shelf in our Sunday School classroom.

Reading, thinking about the Bible's application to my life, writing poetry, and taking a first time stab at song writing was how I filled my days when it was too cold to be outdoors. I read the New Testament story of the Prodigal Son, that stubborn, self-centered boy who left home after insisting that his father give him his inheritance. This was a story that I didn't see as relating to my own life. There were no similarities between myself and the spoiled boy or his jealous brother and I certainly was nothing like the patient, forgiving father. Still, the story made enough of an impression that the first song I ever penned was about that very Bible lesson.

I hadn't set out to write a song. I was upstairs looking out my bedroom window and listening to the rhythm of a rain shower drip, drip, drip, from the roof to the ground. The song came into my head and so I grabbed a pencil and wrote down the lyrics. The entire song was on paper in less than ten minutes, as if I'd been singing it all my life.

Chorus 1   Little child, where are you running to
Little child, where are you going
Don't you know that somebody cares for you?
Come back home, little child

Yesterday you thought that you had everything
Earthly treasures, worldly pleasures, livin' like a king
But now your wealth is gone, those 'friends' deserted you
Maybe what your father said is true

Chorus 2   Little child, where are you going to
Little child, why are you running
Don't you know, this world is too big for you?
Come back home, little child

How can you expect him to keep loving you?
You've lived in shame, you're not the same child that he knew

Wandering 'round in guilt and sin, there's no
place left to roam
Now it's time for you to come back home.

Chorus 3   Little child, why are you wandering
Little child, where are you going
Did you forget that somebody cares for you?
Come back home, little child.

The road back home is longer that you thought
it'd be
Wasted years and bitter tears, such painful
memories
But there He stands with open arms, Oh, what
a joyous day!
It's as though you never went away

Chorus 4   Little child, what were you running from
Little child, where were you going
Don't you know? In love I've forgiven you
Welcome home little child.

I knew that the punctuation was wrong and I had ended sentences with prepositions but that didn't matter. I hadn't written the song for my English teachers. It probably wouldn't sound great to anyone else but me. It was *my* song and I thought it sounded perfect. Along with the words came the melody. I wondered why all of this even entered my mind. I had read so many other Bible stories and the one about the prodigal didn't even make it into my top ten favorites.

Although I didn't have a tape recorder, I never forgot the song. I never changed the lyrics nor the tune and it continued to play in my head from that time forward. If I couldn't remember a lot of other things, I could always recall my little folk song about that wayward child who had to experience life on his own terms and make his own rules before he realized how wrong he was.

While riding the bus to school one morning after Spring Break, I found myself thinking about my dwindling hopes for a third miracle. I thought about how long it had been since I'd asked God to turn the water into wine and how desperate I'd been for some kind of assurance that sainthood awaited me. My hopes had changed a lot in the nine months that had passed since we lived on Maynard Street. And I thought of how right-on-target I was for deciding against becoming a nun.

As the world was heading toward the 1970s, the new fashion in nun-wear was suddenly (and shockingly) skirts and blazers. The ankle length black habits were out of style and now business suits were in. On television I had seen nuns wearing short length headgear that looked more like a scarf than a veil. It looked as if they had just washed their hair and left a dark brown or navy blue towel draped over their head. Some nuns weren't wearing anything on their head nowadays! What had happened to the Catholic Church!?! Where were the traditional vestments that set nuns apart from every other woman in the world? Now, according to my fashion sense, nuns looked like regular people. I didn't even want to think what other changes might be taking place while I was on this extended furlough from the church.

As I looked out the window of the bus, I remembered back to when there wasn't a night that passed without my wondering what had happened to that third miracle. I had imagined that God was never disappointed in me as He observed how I devoted myself to preparing for sainthood. I'd been a good girl. I prayed the prayer book prayers as well as the free-style ones. I was kind to others, obeyed my parents, and I smiled a lot. Sometimes I attempted to reason with Him, admitting that maybe I'd been too young before but now I was more than ready.

On more than one occasion I'd been so bold as to inform God that I felt I was long over-due for whatever it was that was going to make me a saint. Although I never voiced it in prayer, I sometimes thought that if I didn't get my miracle number three during this week or that month, or a particular season of the year, who knows what I might start doing that I shouldn't do. No, I'd never go back to thievery but there are other, equally wrongful things a girl could get herself into if she thought she'd been denied her lifelong ambition.

The thirty minute bus ride finally got us to the high school but we had to stay seated while band members were boarding the bus parked in front of us. They were wearing their uniforms and carrying their instruments. My song came to mind. I could hear the melody and then I imagined myself singing the words. Midway into the verses, I suddenly realized who the song was about. I was the impatient, demanding prodi*gal*. It was *me* who had demanded what I believed to be my inheritance. I was the one who, for nearly seven years, had been informing God of what I thought I had coming to me.

My saint-seeking ways had become a part of the past but I could not deny that I'd been prodigal-like in expecting something that God may not have intended for me. Little by little, it seemed that I had replaced my expectation of being at the top of God's list of favorites with a more reasonable goal: Now I wanted to learn how to become the girl that He created me to be. When I had finally extinguished that self-centered fire inside, that's when God gave me a song. The message of the song let me know that although my ambition was unrealistic, I was not in trouble for having childishly wanted what I'd wanted. I'd been wrong, but He still loved me.

Little child, where were you going?
Don't you know? In love I've forgiven you.
Welcome home little child.

🕊 🕊 🕊

Chapter 20

NEW LIFE

Weather permitting, and if I'd finished my chores and didn't have somewhere else to go, I liked to spend a part of each Saturday or Sunday at Oronogo's claim to fame, the old Circle Cave Mine.

Most folks referred to it as The Circle. It was a beautiful area and I liked the history of it all. There, my grandfather, his brother, and all their friends had mined for ore in the 1920s and 30s. Later, when much of the mine collapsed, water filled the more than four-story high walls of stone. The actual depth of the cave was unknown although scuba divers had made several attempts to determine how far into the earth the center of the pit actually went.

I heard that there had been numerous drownings over the years when divers got pulled under by unexpected vacuum-like currents deep below the surface of the water. Kids at the post office/school bus-stop told me that the bodies of most of the people who drown were never found because The Circle is so deep that eventually no light can get into the pitch black darkness. They said that there are probably a lot of cars and trucks at the bottom of the mine and if you got drunk and drove off the edge of one of the cliffs, you'd never survive; they'd never find you or your car because nobody would want to go looking down there.

I rarely saw other people at The Circle and never bothered to wonder why. A person could find a good sitting spot along the edges of the rocks and stay for hours without being seen by passersby. Actually, there may have been a dozen people at The Circle each time I visited but I didn't see them because the lake area was so big and had so many great hiding places. I had a favorite spot where I could look at the trees that grew up out of the edges of the cliffs. How in the world their roots could grow against the solid rock was a mystery to my unscientific mind.

When I first began visiting The Circle back in September, I would say some of my prayer-book prayers. I'd say them out loud because although there wasn't an echo, the sound was different than anywhere I'd ever been. I especially liked to say the Apostle's Creed because it always caused me to think about people throughout the world having prayed that very prayer for hundreds of years. I thought of it as being very much like the Pledge of Allegiance except that one was for our country and one was for our God.

My praying had changed a lot over the eight-or-so months that had passed. Now my new and improved way of praying was to wake up in the morning and let the first words out of my mouth be "Dear God, thank you for this new day", and then I'd continue to pray impromptu prayers throughout the day until the very last word I'd speak before I went to sleep at night would be "Amen". Instead of a list of prayers, I was now saying one single prayer that started in the morning and ended at night. No one ever gave me the idea to pray that way, I just did it because it seemed to be the way that I was meant to communicate with God. It no longer mattered to me whether or not anyone would approve or disapprove of this behavior. It was between me and God.

With the exception of the coldest winter days, I tried to visit The Circle at least once a week to collect my thoughts and sometimes to organize them into little lists. I might make a list of my favorite words, the best Bible stories, my top favorite slow songs, fast songs, the cutest guys at school. I could break down a list into sub-lists by deciding, for example, the three cutest blue eyed boys, the three cutest brown eyed boys, and then make another list until I was able to come up with my number one favorite guy for that week.

On this one particular Saturday in May, the weather had warmed into the seventies and everything around me looked and felt beautiful. The sun was making an amazing display on the water. It looked as if Someone had sprinkled a straight line of diamonds down the center of the lake. They sparkled in silver, pinkish, yellow and gold against the dark blue and you could see a reflection of the perfectly formed white clouds overhead. There were no fish in this lake because the water was very alkaline, which made it crystal clear. Now and then I would throw a pebble into the water and watch the rings multiply around the spot where it landed.

Just as I was getting comfortable, the same question crossed my mind that had nagged at me during the past several visits. I wondered once again if I would make it into Heaven if I died at that very moment in time. If I fell off the rocks and drown in this bottomless pit of a mining cave, what would happen next? I decided that the list I would make on this day would be of the things that I believed a person needed to do to be guaranteed admission into Heaven.

Before my thinking could shift into new-list mode, it occurred to me how much my beliefs had changed over the years and even more so over the past year. Whereas when I was younger I imagined that entrance into Heaven depended on one's completion of the sacraments of the Catholic Church (or at least six of them if you didn't go for Holy Orders), I now felt certain that this was more a church rule than an actual God-rule. I recalled my belief that unless you'd visited the priest and confessed your sins on the Saturday before your death, said penance, and had every good intention of receiving communion the next day, you were disqualified for residence in Heaven.

I couldn't avoid revisiting the dreams that I'd harbored for so many years about being a nun and then a Catholic saint in order to assure my place in Eternity. At that moment, however, as I gazed out at the diamond studded water, even Holy Orders did not seem powerful enough to qualify me for an eternity in the presence of God.

I began making a mental list of what I believed God would require of me if I were to suddenly find myself standing before Him, dripping wet from an accidental drowning. I thought about all that I had read in the Bible, all that I had heard the priests and the preacher say from the pulpit. I thought about the testimonies of those whom Brother Robison had referred to as saints. My list was surprisingly uncomplicated:

- I need to believe in God, His Son Jesus Christ, and His Holy Spirit.
- I need to accept Him and His Word as The Truth.
- I need to recognize that I've been rebellious, stubborn, sinful, and no better than the Prodigal Son or anyone else, and that
- The only way I can straighten out my crookedness is to live in a way that is pleasing to God.
- I need to be sorry for my sinfulness and I need to go directly to God for His forgiveness.

Everything on my list to that point was doable. If these were the requirements, I was well on my way to satisfying each one. The last item on my list, however, was the hardest to reckon with but it was equally necessary:

- I need to gather up all my self-centered beliefs, everything that I have personally invented about religion to fit my own likes and dislikes. I need to gather all of this into a bundle and go back in my mind to that Garden where Jesus once prayed for me. I need to lay that bundle down beside Him. If

He asked me what it was (even though He would already know the answer), I would say "This is my unworthiness".

I needed to leave that bundle right there at Jesus' feet. Much easier said than done. Why? Because in order to do this, I was going to have to come face-to-face with the differences between my uniquely styled religion (it was not Catholicism, it was Teresaism) and the True belief system that results in living a Heaven-bound life.

Why did this part of the list seem so difficult? I had been raised to leave things behind and to not look back. I knew how to start fresh and how to change my ways. The whole idea of becoming what the world recognizes as a Christian could have been a quick and easy decision for me but something inside of me was insisting that this decision was too important to minimize. I knew that although I could make the decision in an instant, I mustn't. This time it was different. This time, it wasn't someone else's choice that would change my life. It was *my* choice and no one could make it for me. I needed to be absolutely certain that the choice I made was intentional and unchangeable. In that moment, I wanted to push the decision to the back of my mind and to focus, instead, on easier things.

I decided to concentrate on something lighter, something that would make me feel a little better. I thought about what an amazing discovery it was to learn that sainthood isn't something that, if you're lucky enough, falls down from Heaven and lands in your lap. Sainthood isn't something that someone does for you. It is a lifestyle. It's something that you do, that you become by choice. I really loved knowing this and I loved that the whole idea for it comes from the Bible. It took a while for me to figure out, but I finally gained a new and very cool understanding of the word 'servant': I'd discovered that sainthood is the result of servanthood. In order to be a saint, I needed to learn how to be a servant. Wow! Just rethinking this bit of wisdom was almost too much for me to comprehend. Why? Not because it was difficult but because it was so simple, so pure, and so very much what I'd learned by reading my Bible, the Word of God.

I thought about what a wonderful father God had always been to me. He'd sent the gentleman priest to my home to still my shy-yet-smart-aleck, fearful soul. A few months later, He allowed me the opportunity to visit the Catholic Church after so many years of longing. He presented me with the Wasted Life dream. He actually wrote me a song about being His prodigal daughter. And now I would watch, and listen, and learn as He guided me in the direction that I needed to go in order to someday spend an eternity with Him in Heaven.

I was changing. God had not changed. Even with my newly discovered way of loving Him, He was still the God of my childhood, the God of my growing-up, the God of my every breath. My understanding of God as Creator, Father, Savior, and Judge remained consistent through the years and proved to be on target as I learned more about Him. Still yet, it seemed as if I was always searching for Him. How wonderful to finally realize that He was never lost. It was always me who was trying to find my way Home. While everything around me was predictably unpredictable, God was constant. He was the 'for sure', the 'guarantee' that I needed more than honors and awards, more than sainthood. Yes, I was changing.

Sitting in the peace and quiet of that afternoon I tried to concentrate on things that make me feel joyful and lighthearted but my mind kept approaching thoughts that I wanted to avoid. I wanted to look at the beautiful blue of the water and think about how God created so many shades of that one color. Instead, my mind kept going back in time to one dreadful Saturday four years in the past. I kept thinking about sitting in catechism class that morning in 1965 when Sister Mary Francis told us about the Crucifixion.

Why did that day have to surface so powerfully in my mind? I didn't want to hear about it then and I didn't want to think about it now but the memory was crystal clear. I remembered the shafts of sunlight coming through our classroom window and making shadows behind her as she told us about Jesus' death. Her voice kept breaking as if she was trying not to cry. I could tell that she didn't like teaching this part of the catechism. The way she spoke made it seem as if the Crucifixion had just happened the previous day and that she had just received the news. Now, on this Saturday four years later, and nearly two thousand miles down the road, something deep inside of me was saying that it was time to take another look at the day they killed my Jesus.

I stopped looking out at the water. I opened my hand to let the pebbles fall onto the rocks beside me. It was in the Garden of Gethsemane where I had last entered into the presence of my Jesus and now I was going to go to the most difficult place of all, to Calvary. I lowered my head and closed my eyes as I allowed all of the horrible images to resurface. The thoughts came back slowly and in graphic detail. There was the loud noise of the crowd, the whips, the blood, and the nearly unbearable weight of the cross. They even spit on Him. He was hurting and being humiliated. There were the heavy nails and the sound of them being hammered into His hands. Jesus experienced all of this in the same horrible way that any human being would feel excruciating, unrelenting pain. He was being treated like a criminal. He was as human as the people who were torturing Him and yet He was the Son of God. All He had to do was say "stop" and it would have stopped, but He didn't. He didn't make it stop. These thoughts were like loud shrieks in my mind, like someone was screaming or screeching the details of the day He died.

And then the screaming stopped. My mind was quiet and very clear as if someone had turned the pages of a book to one that was absolutely blank. I opened my eyes and in that very instant, I recognized a truth I'd learned so long ago but that I had not taken the time to absorb. The truth was that they didn't cleverly capture and then kill my Jesus – He allowed it all to happen. He chose to be crucified so that the world could be saved from sin. He chose to sacrifice His life so that my life could be saved. Oh, wow.

Jesus died so that in May of 1969 at Circle Cave in Oronogo Missouri, Teresa Elaine Prins could leave her bundled up burden at the foot of the cross and say, "Jesus, I am so sorry". And that is what I did; that is what I said. I said, "Jesus! I am so sorry!" And then, in my heart and in mind I heard His answer as He said "Forgiven". And when I stood to my feet and said out loud, "O, Jesus, Thank You. Thank You for saving me", my heart, my mind and every fiber of my being knew that He said "Saved".

🕊 🕊 🕊

EPILOGUE

I did not grow up to eventually become a world-renown song writer, ha ha. I became the wife of John, and the mother of Jordan David and Jessica Joy.

After earning degrees in Psychology and Human Relations/Counseling, I became a professional counselor-family therapist. Eventually I became a poet, a gardener, a quilter, and the Grandmommie of David Elijah and Raegan Nicole.

I did pen another song, however. As I walked home from The Circle that day in May 1969, God put a melody in my heart. The lyrics seemed very Psalm-like. I sang it aloud and then hurried home to write it down. I was glad that this one was not a song about me. It was a song in praise of what Jesus has done for me, for you, for all of mankind.

Ask me sometime and I'll sing it for you.

🕊 🕊 🕊

Printed in the United States
By Bookmasters